REIKI

The Healing Touch

First and Second Degree Manual

William Lee Rand

Revised and Expanded Edition

Notice to Prospective Students

The ability to channel Reiki energy cannot be learned by reading this manual. This ability is transferred to the student by the Reiki Master during an attunement process. Reiki attunements are given as a standard part of Reiki training. This manual will help those wanting to learn more about Reiki in order to decide if Reiki training is something they would like to take. However, its main purpose is for those who have already taken Reiki or for those preparing to take the training. See "The Attunement" in Chapter 1.

The ideas and techniques described in this manual are for the Reiki student. They are not meant to be an independent guide for self-healing. If you have a health condition and intend to use Reiki, please do so under the supervision of an enlightened medical doctor or other health care professional.

Revised and Expanded Edition
February 1998

ISBN 0-9631567-0-5
Library of Congress Catalog Card Number 98-84919

Published in the United States of America.

Vision Publications
29209 Northwestern Hwy., #592, Southfield, MI 48034
Phone (800) 948-8112, (248) 948-8112 Fax (248) 948-9534
E-mail center@reiki.org Web site www.reiki.org

Acknowledgments

This book would not be possible without the help and encouragement of many. I would like to thank the following Reiki Masters whose loving devotion has contributed to my Reiki training. I am especially grateful to the late Bethal Phaigh, my first Reiki teacher, who through her presence deepened my commitment to serve others. I would also like to thank Diane McCumber for encouraging me to teach Reiki, and Cherie Prasuhn for sharing the information her intense curiosity uncovered. I would also like to thank Harry Kuboi and Beth Gray for sharing their Reiki knowledge and energy while I was living in Hawaii. Arjava Petter and Shuziko Akimoto provided valuable information on the history of Reiki. I also wish to thank my Reiki spirit guides who send their love, wisdom and healing whenever it is needed.

I acknowledge all Reiki practitioners and teachers for the contributions they are making to end suffering and heal humanity.

Cover Art and Illustrations
Sheryl M. Matsko

Modeling
Connie Greba

Editing
Susan A. Martin

Typesetting
Bonnie J. Hall

The Logo

The Japanese kanji in the center of the logo means Reiki which is spiritually guided life energy. The upward pointing triangle represents humanity moving toward God. The downward pointing triangle represents God moving toward humanity. Because the two triangles are united, and balanced, they represent humanity and God working together in harmony. The inner sixteen petaled flower symbolizes the throat chakra or communication. The outer twelve petaled flower symbolizes the heart chakra or love. The complete logo represents Reiki uniting God and humanity in harmony through the communication of love.

William Lee Rand has lived in Hawaii, California and Michigan. He has a broad background in metaphysics including twenty years of experience as a hypnotherapist. He has specialized in past-life regression therapy and spiritual development. He is also a former Rosicrucian, professional astrologer and tarot card reader, and is certified in Neuro-Linguistic Programming by the Robbins Research Institute. While living in Hawaii, he worked with a Kahuna. He is founder of The International Center for Reiki Training in Southfield, Michigan, and is the publisher of the *Reiki News*. He has written over forty articles on Reiki and recorded and produced seven audio tapes.

In 1981, William took First Degree Reiki from Bethal Phaigh on the Big Island of Hawaii. Bethal was one of Takata's original Master's and in 1982, he took Second Degree Reiki from Bethal. William received the Reiki Master attunement and training from Reiki Masters Diane McCumber and Marlene Schilke in 1989, Reiki Master Cherie Prasuhn in 1990 and Reiki Master Leah Smith in 1992. William has also reviewed Reiki I and II with Phyllis Furumoto. Always seeking to learn more, his research into Reiki is an ongoing process. His recent trip to Japan has helped confirm new information about the history of Reiki which is featured in this book. William teaches Reiki full time in classes world-wide.

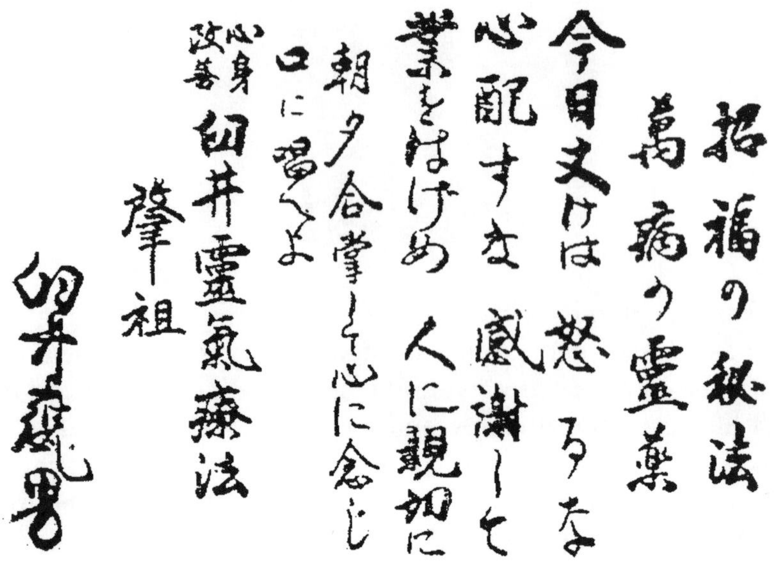

The Original Reiki Ideals

The secret art of inviting happiness
The miraculous medicine of all diseases
Just for today, do not be angry
Do not worry and be filled with gratitude
Devote yourself to your work and be kind to people
Every morning and evening join your hands in prayer,
pray these words to your heart,
and chant these words with your mouth
Usui Reiki Treatment for the improvement of body and mind

The founder . . . Usui Mikao

Table of Contents

Part I - An Overview of Reiki

Appendices

Appendix A - Discovering the Roots of Reiki

Appendix B - Reiki in Hospitals

Appendix C - Reiki Training and Licensing
through the International Center for Reiki Training

Part I

An Overview of Reiki

靈氣

Chapter 1
Reiki Defined

Reiki (pronounced *ray-key*) is a Japanese technique for stress reduction and relaxation that also promotes healing. It was rediscovered by Dr. Mikao Usui in the early 1900's. Reiki is administered by "laying on of hands" and techniques such as this have been practiced for thousands of years. Reiki is a very simple yet powerful technique that can be easily learned by anyone.

The word Reiki comes from two Japanese words - *Rei* and *Ki*. They are shown on the opposite page. Rei is the upper character and Ki is the lower character.

Rei - Spiritual Wisdom

The word "Rei" means universal and this is the definition most have accepted. However, this interpretation is a very general one. Japanese ideograms have many levels of meaning. They vary from the mundane to the highly esoteric. So, while it is true that Rei can be interpreted as universal, meaning that it is present everywhere, there is a more meaningful definition that is worth exploring.

Research into the esoteric meaning of the Japanese kanji character for Rei has given a much deeper understanding of this ideogram. The word Rei as it is used in Reiki is more accurately interpreted to mean higher knowledge or spiritual consciousness. This is the wisdom that comes from God or the Higher Self and is the God-Consciousness which is all-knowing. It understands each person completely. It knows the cause of all problems and difficulties and knows how to heal them.

Ki - Life Energy

The word "Ki" means the same as *Chi* in Chinese, *Prana* in Sanskrit and *Ti* or *Ki* in Hawaiian. It has also been called odic force, orgone and bioplasma. It has been given many other names in various cultures.

Ki is life energy. It is also known as the vital life force or the universal life force. This is the non-physical energy that animates all living things. As long as something is alive, it has life energy circulating through it and surrounding it; when it dies, the life energy departs. If your life energy is low, or if there is a restriction in its flow, you are more vulnerable to illness. When it is high, and flowing freely, you are less likely to get sick. Life energy plays an important role in everything we do. It animates the body and has higher levels of expression. Ki is also the primary energy of our emotions, thoughts and spiritual life.

The Chinese place great importance on life energy, or Chi. They have studied it for thousands of years and have discovered there are many different kinds of Chi. The *Yellow Emperor's Classic of Internal Medicine*, which is over 4,000 years old, lists thirty-two different kinds of Chi or Ki.

Ki is used by martial artists in their physical training and mental development. It is used in meditative breathing exercises called pranayama, and by the shamans of all cultures for divination, psychic awareness, manifestation and healing. Ki is the non-physical energy used by all healers. Ki is present all around us and can be accumulated and guided by the mind. Russian researcher Semyon Kirlian developed a method in the 1940's for photographing the field of life energy that surrounds a person (see end of this chapter).

Spiritually Guided Life Energy

It is the God-Consciousness called Rei that *guides* the life energy called Ki in the practice we call Reiki. Therefore, Reiki can be defined as spiritually guided life energy. This is a meaningful interpretation of the word Reiki. It more closely describes the experience most people have of it; Reiki guiding itself with its own wisdom, rather than requiring the direction of the practitioner.

Do All Healers Use Reiki?

There are many kinds of healing energy. All healing energy has Ki or life energy as one of its important parts. All healers use life energy or Ki, but not all use Reiki. Reiki is a special kind of healing energy that can only be channeled by someone that has been attuned to it. Reiki is life energy that is guided by the Higher Power. While it is possible that some people are born with Reiki or have gotten it some other way, most people need to receive a Reiki attunement to be able to use Reiki. Therefore, most healers who have not received the Reiki attunement from a Reiki Master are not using Reiki but another kind of healing energy. Healers who have not taken a Reiki class can benefit from doing so. People who already do healing work report a consistent increase of at least fifty percent in the strength of their healing energies after taking the Reiki training.

This was verified for me when I first began teaching Reiki. Two clairvoyant healers I knew who had highly developed abilities decided to take Reiki training from me. They could easily see the life energy flowing through a person's body, as well as see the aura and chakras. They could communicate with a person's guides and Higher Self. They were adept at moving negative psychic energy out of the body as well as channeling healing energies. In my twenty years of metaphysical work, they were the most accurate and effective psychic healers I had met.

These healers later told me they had doubted there was anything I was teaching they couldn't already do, but they had taken the Reiki training simply to support me in my new work. After the attunement, they were amazed at the difference between the healing energies they had been using and Reiki. They said the Reiki energies were more powerful and of a much higher frequency. Also Reiki didn't have to be guided like the other healing energies they were using, and the Reiki energies began flowing without having to enter an altered state. The attunement process itself was a powerful healing experience for them, releasing restrictions relating to their healing work that they had unknowingly acquired as healers in past lives. They were very pleased they had taken the class.

The Attunement

Reiki is not taught in the way other healing techniques are taught. The ability is transferred to the student by the Reiki Master during an attunement process. During the attunement, the Rei or God-Consciousness makes adjustments in the student's chakras and energy pathways to accommodate the ability to channel Reiki and then links the student ot the source of Reiki. These changes are unique for each person. The attunement energies are channeled into the student through the Reiki Master. The Reiki Master does not direct the process and is simply a channel for the attunement energy flowing from the Higher Power.

The Reiki attunement is a powerful spiritual experience for most people. The process is guided by the Rei or God-Consciousness, which makes adjustments in the process depending on the needs of each student. The attunement is also attended by Reiki guides and other spiritual beings who help implement the process. Many report having mystical experiences involving personal messages, healings, visions and past-life experiences. The attunement can also increase psychic sensitivity. Students often report an opening of the third eye, increased intuitive awareness or other psychic experiences after receiving a Reiki attunement.

Once you have received a Reiki attunement, you will have Reiki for the remainder of your life. It does not wear off and you can never lose it. While one attunement per level is all that is necessary to activate the ability to channel Reiki, additional attunements to levels already attained prove beneficial. These benefits include refinement of the Reiki energy one is channeling, increased strength of the energy, healing of personal problems, clarity of mind, increased psychic sensitivity and a raised level of consciousness. At the Reiki support groups sponsored by the International Center for Reiki Training, additional attunements are usually given at no extra charge by someone who is a Reiki Master.

A Cleansing Process

The Reiki attunement can start a cleansing process that affects the physical body as well as the mind and emotions. Toxins that have been stored in the body may be released along with feelings and thought patterns that are no longer useful. This does not always take place after a Reiki attunement, but when it does, it is important to understand what is happening so you can support its completion. Whenever change takes place, even if it is good, a period of adjustment is necessary so that the body and various parts of your life can get used to the healthy new conditions. You may need more rest, and it can also be helpful to spend more time quietly contemplating your life and any changes you might need to make to support a healthier lifestyle. Many have found that a process of purification prior to and after the attunement improves the benefit one receives. Please refer to Appendix C for specific instructions on preparing for an attunement.

Giving Reiki

After the attunement, all that is necessary for practitioners to use Reiki is to place their hands on the "person to be healed" with the intention of healing. The Reiki energies will begin flowing automatically. Reiki has its own intelligence and knows exactly where to go and what to do. It is not necessary to direct the Reiki. It will communicate with the client's Higher Self and use this information to decide where to go and what to do. The best results are achieved by simply remaining calm and relaxed and enjoying the soothing energies that are flowing through you.

Reiki Can Never Cause Harm

Because Reiki is guided by God-Consciousness, it can never do harm. It always knows what a person needs and will adjust itself to create an effect that is appropriate. One never need worry about whether to give Reiki or not. It is always helpful.

In addition, because the practitioner does not direct the healing and does not decide what to work on, or what to heal, the practitioner is not in danger of taking on the karma of the client. Because the practitioner is not doing the healing, it is also much easier for the ego to stay out of the way and allow the presence of God to clearly shine through.

Reiki Never Depletes Your Energy

Because it is a channeled healing, the Reiki practitioner's energies are never depleted. In fact, the Reiki consciousness considers both practitioner and client to be in need of healing, so both receive treatment. Because of this, giving a treatment always increases one's energy and leaves one surrounded with loving feelings of well-being.

Anyone Can Learn Reiki

The ability to learn Reiki is not dependent on intellectual capacity, nor does one have to be able to meditate. It does not take years of practice. It is simply passed on from the teacher to the student. As soon as this happens, one has Reiki and can use it. Because of this, it is easily learned by anyone.

Reiki is a pure form of healing not dependent on individual talent or acquired ability. Because of this, the personality of the healer is less likely to cloud the significance of the experience. The feeling of being connected directly to God's healing love and protection is clearly apparent.

Self-Treatment

In addition to using Reiki on others, you can also treat yourself. This is one of the wonderful advantages of Reiki. It works just as well on yourself as it does on others. Complete instruction is given in the Reiki training for self-treatment. Chapter 6 shows the standard hand positions necessary to give yourself a complete Reiki treatment.

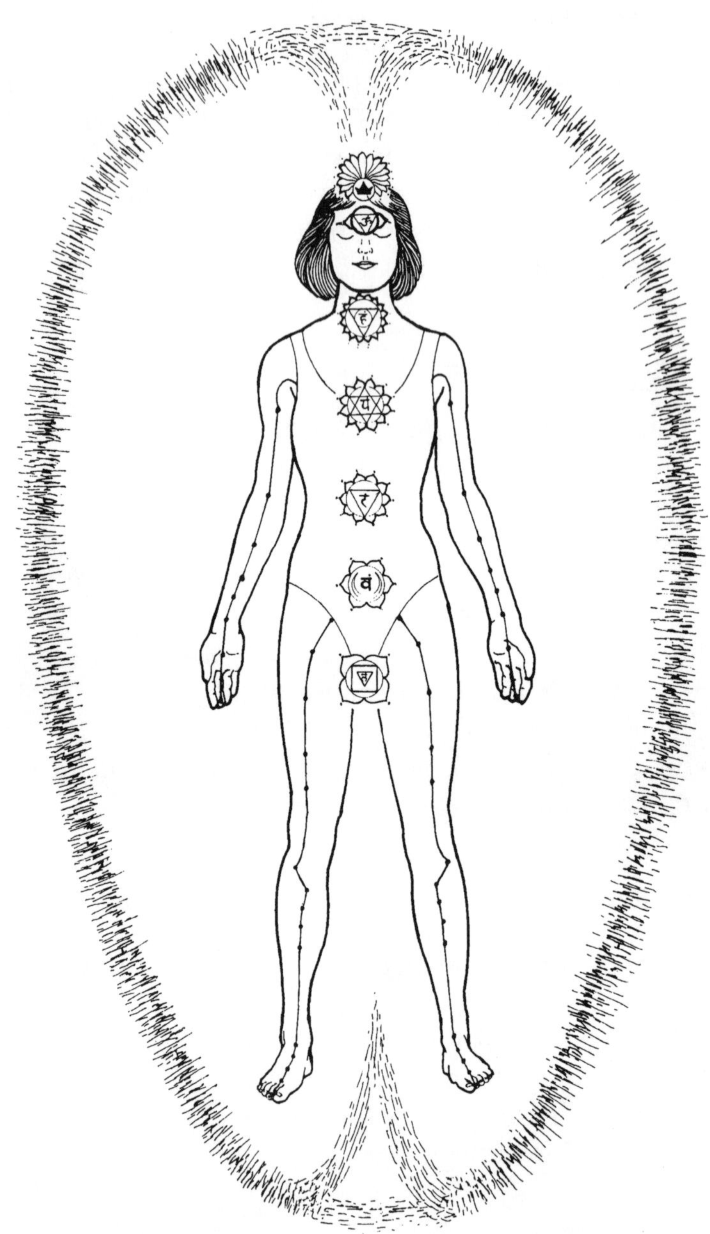

The human subtle energy system, showing the primary chakras and a portion of the Aura and Meridian system

How Does Reiki Heal?

We are alive because life energy or Ki is flowing through us. Ki flows within the physical body through pathways called chakras, meridians and nadis. It also flows around us in a field of energy called the aura. The free and balanced flow of Ki is the cause of health. It is Ki that animates the physical organs and tissues as it flows through them. Ki nourishes the organs and cells of the body, supporting them in their vital functions. When the flow of Ki is disrupted, it interferes with the healthy functioning of one or more of the organs and tissues of the physical body. Therefore, it is the disruption in the flow of Ki that is the main cause of illness.

Ki is responsive to thoughts and feelings. When we have positive optimistic thoughts, we increase our flow of Ki and this causes us to feel better. However, when we have negative thoughts, our Ki is disrupted and diminished and we do not feel as good. When negative thoughts become lodged in the subconscious mind, they create a permanent disruption of Ki. This happens when we either consciously or unconsciously accept negative thoughts or feelings about ourselves. These negative thoughts and feelings attach themselves to the energy field and disrupt the flow of Ki. Various organs and tissues of the body can be affected depending on the site of the blockage. This diminishes the vital function of those organs and cells of the physical body and unless the blockage is released, a person could eventually become ill.

When a person receives a Reiki treatment, the Rei or God-Conscious part of the energy assesses where the person has blocks and then directs the healing energy, usually to the block that is nearest the hands. However, sometimes it will go to the block that is most important even if it is far from the hands. The Reiki energy then works with the negative thoughts and feelings that are blocking one's natural flow of Ki and heals them as well. This can happen in a number of ways. By flowing through the affected parts of the energy field and charging them with positive energy, Reiki raises the vibratory level in and around the physical body where the negative thoughts and feelings are attached. This causes the negative energy to break apart and fall away. In so doing, Reiki clears, straightens and heals the energy pathways, thus allowing healthy Ki to flow in a natural way. Sometimes the entire blocking energy is lifted up to a higher field of energy where it is processed. Other times, it is melted away or burned up. When a block is released, sometimes a person will feel a cold sensation and when it is melted or burned up, a hot sensation. Once Ki is flowing naturally, the physical organs and tissues are then able to complete their healing process.

What Can Be Treated?

Reiki is both powerful and gentle. In its long history of use it has aided in healing virtually every known illness and injury including serious problems like multiple sclerosis, heart disease, and cancer as well as skin problems, cuts, bruises, broken bones, headaches, colds, flu, sore throat, sunburn, fatigue, insomnia and impotence. It is always beneficial and works to improve the effectiveness of all other types of therapy. A treatment feels like a wonderful glowing radiance and has many benefits for both client and practitioner, including positive states of consciousness and spiritual experiences.

Reiki works in harmony with all other kinds of treatment. You need not limit yourself to receiving Reiki by itself. In fact, if you have a health condition and want to be treated with Reiki, it is recommended that you do so under the supervision of an enlightened medical doctor or other health care professional.

Reiki Can Be Complementary

You can continue to receive regular medical or psychological treatment while receiving Reiki, with improved results. In fact, Reiki will improve the results of any medical treatment, acting to reduce negative side effects, such as those from chemotherapy, surgery and invasive procedures. It shortens healing time, reduces or eliminates pain, reduces stress and helps create optimism. It has been regularly noted that patients receiving Reiki leave the hospital earlier than those who don't.

Reiki has also been used in conjunction with psychotherapy to improve the healing of emotional trauma and other issues. Its psychological benefits can include improved memory and greater self-confidence. If clients have a physical or psychological condition and want to be treated with Reiki, it is recommended that they do so under the supervision of an enlightened medical doctor, psychologist or other health care professional.

Is Reiki a Religion?

While Reiki is spiritual in nature, it is not a religion. It has no dogma, and there is nothing you must believe in order to learn and use Reiki. In fact, Reiki is not dependent on belief at all and will work whether you believe in it or not. Because Reiki comes from God, it enables many people to go beyond intellectual concepts and directly experience their religion.

Kirlian Photography

Kirlian photography is a technique of photographing the etheric energy patterns around living things. Pioneered by Semyon Kirlian, a Russian researcher in the 1940's, it is based on a phenomenon known as corona discharge. When an object is in a high-frequency electrical field and becomes grounded, a spark discharges between the object and the electrode. A piece of film is placed between the object and the electrode and the discharge pattern is captured on the film. When a living thing is used as the object, beautiful colors and patterns are created on the film. This discharge pattern seems to follow the pattern of the etheric aura.

Reiki Photograph

The Kirlian photograph on the next page was taken in May of 1990 by Doris Kangas. Doris asked me to be a subject for the Kirlian process to determine if Reiki energy could be detected. Her process involves taking fingerprint Kirlian photos with a Polaroid film device inside a black bag. Three sets of fingertip photos were taken on the same film. The first three fingers of my right hand were used. During the first two photos I just sat calmly. During the last photo, which is the set of prints at the bottom, I placed my left hand on my leg and asked Reiki to flow. I also asked my Reiki guides to assist in the process. When I felt a strong flow of Reiki out of my right hand, I told Doris I was ready and she took the picture.

Doris has taken hundreds of Kirlian photos and this was the first time she took one that looked like this. It shows Reiki energy emanating from the palm chakra. One beam can be seen to emerge between the thumb and forefinger, and the main beam between the forefinger and middle finger. In the original color photo, the beams are white in the middle, turning blue/white on the edges and indigo at the bottom.

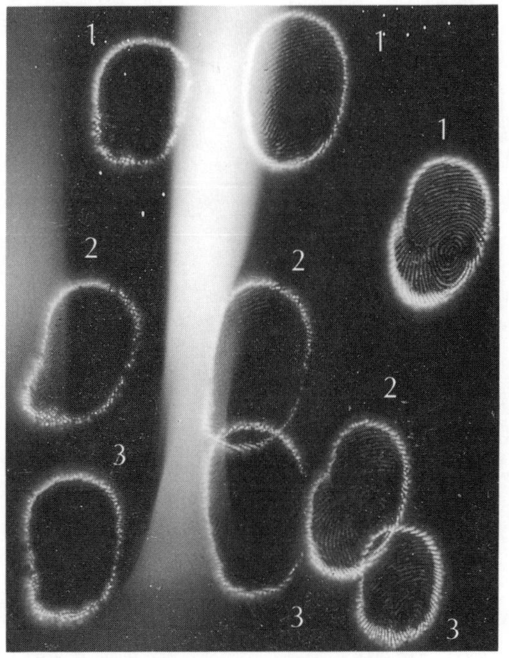

Kirlian photo of Reiki energy

Chapter 2
Reiki Past and Present

Mrs. Hawayo Takata brought Reiki from Japan to the West in 1938. Because of her loving devotion, Reiki has been passed on to more than a million people all over the world, and the numbers continue to grow! Until recently, the only information we had about the history of Reiki came from Mrs. Takata. Her story of Reiki was recorded on tape, and this recording is still available along with a transcript of the contents.[1] Most people including authors have simply accepted this Western interpretation of the history of Reiki as accurate without attempting to do any additional research. Because of this, we find Mrs. Takata's version of the story repeated in most of the current books on Reiki.

In the course of researching the origins of Reiki, I have learned that Mrs. Takata took liberties with the history of its development. In 1990, for example, I wrote to Doshisha University in Kyoto, where Mrs. Takata reported that the founder of Reiki, Usui Sensei, had held the office of president. I had hoped to gain additional information that would help us understand who Usui Sensei really was. I also contacted the University of Chicago, from which Usui Sensei had obtained a degree according to Mrs. Takata. Neither university had ever heard of him. (Copies of the letters from both Universities are available from the International Center for Reiki Training.) This disappointing discovery led me to wonder if other parts of the accepted Takata history of Reiki were also inaccurate. In talking with several early Reiki Masters about this discovery, I was told that Mrs. Takata had Westernized the story of Reiki by changing certain details and adding others to make it more appealing to Americans.

I continued to seek additional information about the history of Reiki, but attempts to secure it went slowly at first. Finally in 1996 I received from Japan a copy of the Original Reiki Ideals, which were different and more interesting than what had been presented by Mrs. Takata. These appear in the front of the book. They include the idea that chanting and offering prayers are important to Reiki practice.[2] Since that time, there have been many other breakthroughs. During a recent trip to Japan, Laura Gifford and I uncovered many new and verifiable facts not formerly known in the West about the origins of Reiki. These new discoveries add vitality to the practice of Reiki and provide a strong verifiable connection to its roots. (See Appendix A, "Discovering the Roots of Reiki," and the inscription on the Usui Memorial below.)

A More Accurate History of Reiki

The following is a new version of the history of Reiki based on recent discoveries. Where possible, sources have been referenced so others can follow up on this research if desired. The history begins with a look at the inscription from a memorial stone which was erected in 1927 in memory of Dr. Mikao Usui, founder of the Reiki healing system.

The Inscription on the Usui Memorial

The inscription on the Usui Memorial, dating from 1927, was written in old Japanese by Mr. Okata, a member of the Usui Shiki Reiki Ryoho, and by Mr. Ushida, who succeeded Usui Sensei as president of the society. The English translation of the inscription is reprinted here from *Reiki Fire* with permission from the author Frank Arjava Petter.

The large kanji at the top of the ten-by-four-foot memorial stone reads: "Memorial of Usui Sensei's Virtue." The remainder of the inscription reads as follows:

> *Someone who studies hard (i.e., practices meditation) and works assiduously to improve body and mind for the sake of becoming a better person is called "a man of great spirit." People who use that great spirit for a social purpose, that is, to teach the right way to many people and do collective good, are called "teachers." Dr. Usui was one such teacher. He taught the Reiki of the universe (universal energy). Countless people asked him to teach them the great way of Reiki and to heal them.*
>
> *Dr. Usui was born in the first year of the Keio period, called Keio Gunnen, on August 15th (1865). His first name was Mikao and his other name was pronounced either Gyoho or Kyoho. He was born in the village of Yago in the Yamagata district of Gifu prefecture. His ancestor's name was Tsunetane Chiba. His father's name was Uzaemon. His mother's family name was Kaweai. From what is known, he was a talented and hard working student. As an adult he traveled to several Western countries and*

Usui Memorial

China to study, worked arduously, but did at [one] point run into some bad luck. However, he didn't give up and trained himself arduously.

One day he went to Mount Kurama on a twenty-one-day retreat to fast and meditate. At the end of this period he suddenly felt the great Reiki energy at the top of his head, which led to the Reiki healing system. He first used Reiki on himself, then tried it on his family. Since it worked well for various ailments, he decided to share this knowledge with the public at large. He opened a clinic in Harajuku, Aoyama, Tokyo in April of the 11th year of the Taisho period (1922). He not only gave treatments to countless patients, some of whom had come from far and wide, but he also hosted workshops to spread his knowledge. In September of the twelfth year of the Taisho period (1923), the devastating Kanto earthquake shook Tokyo. Thousands were killed, injured, or became sick in its aftermath. Dr. Usui grieved for his people, but he also took Reiki to the devastated city and used its healing powers on the surviving victims. His clinic soon became too small to handle the throng of patients, so in February of the 14th year of the Taisho period (1925), he built a new one outside Tokyo in Nakano.

His fame spread quickly all over Japan, and invitations to distant towns and villages started coming in. Once he went to Kure, another time to Hiroshima prefecture, then to Saga prefecture and Fukuyama. It was during his stay in Fukuyama that he was hit by a fatal stroke on March 9th, of the fifteenth year of the Taisho period (1926). He was 62 years of age.

Dr. Usui had a wife named Sadako; her maiden name was Suzuki. They had a son and a daughter. The son, Fuji Usui, took over the family business after Dr. Usui's passing.

Dr. Usui was a very warm, simple and humble person. He was physically healthy and well-proportioned. He never showed off and always had a smile on his face; he was also very courageous in the face of adversity. He was, at the same time, a very cautious person. His talents were many. He liked to read, and his knowledge of medicine, psychology, fortune telling and theology of religions around the world was vast. This lifelong habit of studying and gathering information certainly helped pave the way to perceiving and understanding Reiki. Reiki not only heals diseases, but also amplifies innate abilities, balances the spirit, makes the body healthy, and thus helps achieve happiness. To teach this to others you should follow the five principles of the Meiji Emperor and contemplate them in your heart. They should be spoken daily, once in the morning and once in the evening.

1) Don't get angry today. 2) Don't worry today. 3) Be grateful today. 4) Work hard today (meditative practice). 5) Be kind to others today.

The ultimate goal is to understand the ancient secret method for gaining happiness (Reiki) and thereby discover an all-purpose cure for many ailments. If these principles are followed you will achieve the great tranquil mind of the ancient sages. To begin spreading the Reiki system, it is important to start from a place close to you (yourself), don't start from something distant such as philosophy or logic.

Sit still and in silence every morning and every evening with your hands folded in the 'Ghasso' or 'Namaste'. Follow the great principles, and be clean and quiet. Work on your heart and do things from the quiet space inside of you. Anyone can access Reiki, because it begins within yourself!

Philosophical paradigms are changing the world. If Reiki can be spread throughout the world it will touch the human heart and the morals of society. It will be helpful for many people, not only healing disease, but the Earth as a whole. Over 2,000 people learned Reiki from Dr. Usui. Even more learned from his senior disciples who carried Reiki further. Now after Dr. Usui's passing, Reiki will continue to spread far and wide. It is a universal blessing to have received Reiki from Dr. Usui and to be able to pass it on to others. Many of Dr. Usui's students converged to build this memorial here at Saihoji Temple in the Toyotoma district.

I was asked to write these words to help keep his great work alive. I deeply appreciate his work and I would like to say to all of his disciples that I am honored to have been chosen for this task. May many understand what a great service Dr. Usui did for the world.

Dr. Mikao Usui ("Usui Sensei"),
founder of the Reiki System of Healing

Dr. Mikao Usui

Dr. Mikao Usui, or Usui Sensei as he is called by his students in Japan, was born August 15, 1865 in the village of Yago in the Yamagata district of Gifu prefecture, Japan.[3] It is thought that he entered a Tendai Buddhist school on or near Mt. Kurama ("horse saddle mountain") at age four. He also studied *kiko,* the Japanese version of *qigong,* which is a health and healing discipline based on the development and use of life energy. The young Usui found that these healing methods required the practitioner to build up and then deplete his own life energy when giving treatments. He wondered if it were possible to do healing work without depleting one's own energy.[4]

Usui Sensei had an avid interest in learning and worked hard at his studies. He traveled to Europe and China to further his education. His curriculum included medicine, psychology, and religion as well as fortune telling, which Asians have long considered to be a worthy skill.[5] It is thought that he was from a wealthy family, as in Japan only the wealthy could afford to send their children to school. Eventually he became the secretary to Pei Gotoushin, head of the department of health and welfare who later became the Mayor of Tokyo. The connections Usui Sensei made at this job helped him to become a successful businessman.[6] Usui Sensei was also a member of the Rei Jyutu Ka, a metaphysical group dedicated to developing psychic abilities.[7]

In 1914 Usui's personal and business life was failing.[8] As a sensitive spiritualist, Usui Sensei had spent much time meditating at power spots on Mt. Kurama where he had received his early Buddhist training. So he decided to travel to this holy mountain, where he enrolled in Isyu Guo, a twenty-one-day training course sponsored by the Tendai Buddhist Temple located there.[9] We do not know for certain what he was required to do during this training, but it is likely that fasting, meditation, chanting and prayers were part of the practice. In addition, we know there is a small waterfall on Mt. Kurama where even today people go to meditate. This meditation involves standing under the waterfall and allowing the waters to strike and flow over the top of the head, a practice which is said to activate the crown chakra. Japanese Reiki Masters think that Usui Sensei may have used this meditation as part of his practice. In any case, it was during the Isyu Guo training that the great Reiki energy entered his crown chakra. This greatly enhanced his healing abilities and he realized he had received a wonderful new gift - the ability to give healing to others without depleting his own energy![10]

Interesting parallels exist between the System of Healing Usui Sensei created and some of the symbols and philosophy practiced by the Kurama-Koyo Buddhists (formerly the Tendai Buddhists on Mt. Kurama. (See Appendix A.)

Usui Sensei used his new healing ability to help others, and for the next seven years he worked with the poor people of Kyoto.[11] In 1922, he moved to Tokyo and started a healing society which he named Usui Shiki Reiki Ryoho, which means "The Usui System of Reiki Healing." He also opened a Reiki clinic in Harajuku, Aoyama, Tokyo. There he taught classes and gave treatments.[12] He initially created three degrees for his training which he called *Shoden* (First Degree), *Okuden* (Inner Teaching) and *Shinpiden* (Mystery Teaching).[13] According to Fumio Ogawa, a current member of the Usui Shiki Reiki Ryoho, Usui Sensei had an additional three degrees for a total of six.[14] However, contrary to rumors, Usui Sensei had only four symbols, the same four we use in the West. This fact has been verified by Fumio Ogawa and other members of the Usui Shiki Reiki Ryoho.

Several sources indicate that at first Usui Sensei had no formal attunement process. The student received the ability to do Reiki simply by spending time with Usui Sensei, with the student intending to gain the ability and Usui Sensei intending that the student receive it. It was only after the Reiki movement grew, making it impractical for him to teach in such a personal way, that a formal attunement process similar to what we use today was developed. An interesting note is that Arjava Petter, author of the book *Reiki Fire,* received a Reiki attunement from a Reiki teacher belonging to the Usui Shiki Reiki Ryoho that was remarkably different than what we are familiar with in the West. He said the teacher simply sang poetic songs while Arjava was sitting in front of him, and after a while Arjava felt a tremendous energy come over him.

In 1923, the great Kanto earthquake devastated Tokyo. More than 140,000 people died and over half of the houses and buildings were shaken down or burned. An overwhelming number of people were left homeless, injured, sick and grieving.[15] Usui Sensei felt great compassion for the people and began treating as many as he could with Reiki. This was a tremendous amount of work. Demand for Reiki became so great that he outgrew his clinic, so in 1925 he built a bigger one in Nakano, Tokyo. Because of this, his reputation as a healer spread all over Japan. He began to travel so he could teach and treat more people. During his travels across Japan he directly taught more than 2,000 students and initiated sixteen teachers.[16] The Japanese government issued him a *Kun San To* award for doing honorable work to help others.[17] While teaching in Fukuyama, he suffered a stroke and died on March 9, 1926.[18] His grave is at Saihoji Temple, in Suginami, Tokyo, although some claim that his ashes are located elsewhere.

There were many hands-on healing schools in Japan at the time Usui started his school. These other schools were not part of Usui Reiki.[19] There may have been some connection between Reiki and MahaKari and Johrei as these two Japanese religions have healing as their central purpose and also use the Usui master symbol in their practices.[20]

After Usui Sensei died, his students erected a memorial next to his gravestone. (This is the memorial pictured on page I-17 and described beginning on page I-18.) After Usui died, Mr. J. Ushida took over as president of the Usui Shiki Reiki Ryoho. Mr. Ushida was responsible for creating and erecting the Usui Memorial stone and ensuring that the grave site would be maintained. Mr. Ushida was followed by Mr. Iichi Taketomi, Mr. Yoshiharu Watanabe, Mr. Toyoichi Wanami and the current successor to Usui Sensei, Ms. Kimiko Koyama. She lives in Tokyo and at the age of 92, continues to maintain a Reiki practice. Contrary to what we have been told in the West, there is no "lineage bearer" or "Grand Master" of the organization started by Usui Sensei, only the succession of presidents listed above.[21]

The sixteen teachers initiated by Usui Sensei include Toshihiro Eguchi, Jusaburo Guida, Ilichi Taketomi, Toyoichi Wanami, Yoshiharu Watanabe, Keizo Ogawa, J. Ushida and Chujiro Hayashi.[22] Contrary to one version of the Reiki story, Chujiro Hayashi was not the successor to Usui Sensei, but rather Mr. J. Ushida as previously mentioned. However, Chujiro Hayashi was a respected Master and had his own Reiki school and clinic in Tokyo. He kept records of his treatments and had printed class manuals. (We have a copy of one of Dr. Hayashi's class manuals on file and have translated it. It is a listing of various illnesses and conditions and the Reiki hand positions to treat them.) He practiced and taught Reiki classes and many of his students received their Reiki training in return for working in his clinic.[23] It was to this clinic that Mrs. Takata was directed in 1935.

At the time of this writing, this is all the verifiable information we have concerning how Usui Sensei rediscovered Reiki. There are a number of other interesting stories and some additional information that we have received on the subject, and as it is verified we will pass it on in future editions of this book as well as in our newsletter and at our web site. Researching the story of Reiki is an unfolding adventure for many, and new facts are bound to be discovered that will add to our understanding.

Hawayo Takata

The following is Mrs. Hawayo Takata's version of her early years leading up to her contact with Reiki at the Hayashi clinic:

> *She stated that she was born on December 24th, 1900, on the island of Kauai, Hawaii. Her parents were Japanese immigrants and her father worked in the sugar cane fields. She eventually married the bookkeeper of the plantation where she was employed. His name was Saichi Takata and they had two daughters. In October 1930 Saichi died at the age of 34, leaving Mrs. Takata to raise their two children.*
>
> *In order to provide for her family, she had to work very hard with little rest. After five years she developed severe abdominal pain and a lung condition, and she had a nervous breakdown. Soon after this one of her sisters died and it was Hawayo's*

responsibility to travel to Japan, where her parents had resettled, to deliver the news. She also felt she could receive help for her health in Japan.

After informing her parents, she entered a hospital and stated that she was diagnosed with a tumor, gallstones, appendicitis and asthma.[24] *She was told to prepare for an operation but opted to visit Dr. Hayashi's clinic instead.*

Mrs. Takata was unfamiliar with Reiki but was impressed that the diagnosis of Reiki practitioners at the clinic closely matched the doctor's at the hospital. She began receiving treatments. Two Reiki practitioners would treat her each day. The heat from their hands was so strong, she said, that she thought they were secretly using some kind of equipment. Seeing the large sleeves of the Japanese kimono worn by one, she thought she had found the secret place of concealment. Grabbing his sleeves one day she startled the practitioner, but, of course, found nothing. When she explained what she was doing, he began to laugh and then told her about Reiki and how it worked.

Mrs. Takata got progressively better and in four months was completely healed. She wanted to learn Reiki for herself. In the spring of 1936 she received First Degree Reiki from Dr. Hayashi. She then worked with him for a year and received Second Degree Reiki. Mrs. Takata returned to Hawaii in 1937, followed shortly thereafter by Dr. Hayashi and his daughter who came to help establish Reiki there. In February of 1938 Dr. Hayashi initiated Hawayo Takata as a Reiki Master.

No Postage
Necessary
If Mailed
In The
United States

Business Reply Mail

First Class Permit No. 599, Southfield, MI

Postage will be paid by Addressee

The Center for Reiki Training
29209 Northwestern Hwy., #592
Southfield, MI 48034-9841

Send for a **Free** copy of

Reiki News

and a

Catalog of Reiki Products

T-Shirts, Reiki books, Reiki tapes, class schedule, and more!

Name ______________________________

Address ____________________________

City _______________________________

State ______________ Zip __________ Date ____________

Phone Home (   ) __________ Work (   ) __________

I have already taken ☐ Reiki I ☐ Reiki II ☐ Master

☐ I am interested in attending a Reiki class

To summarize Mrs. Takata's Reiki background, she traveled from Hawaii to Japan to attend her sister's funeral and to visit her parents. Having been diagnosed with several ailments, the main one being asthma, she was guided to Dr. Hayashi's clinic in Tokyo and after receiving four months of Reiki treatments was completely cured.[25] She wanted to learn Reiki in order to continue treating herself and also take it back to Hawaii to share with others. Dr. Hayashi allowed her to work at his clinic and also began giving her Reiki training. She eventually received the *Shinpiden* level which is what we call Reiki Master in the West. Dr. Hayashi officially acknowledged this in Hawaii on February 21, 1938, and also stated that she was one of thirteen Reiki Masters trained by him.[26]

Mrs. Takata practiced Reiki in Hawaii, establishing several clinics, one of which was located in Hilo on the Big Island. She gave treatments and initiated students up to Reiki II. She became a well known healer and traveled to the U.S. mainland and other parts of the world teaching and giving treatments. She was a powerful healer who attributed her success to the fact that she did so much Reiki on each client. She would often do multiple treatments, each sometimes lasting hours, and she often initiated members of a client's family so they could give Reiki to the client as well.

It was not until 1970 that Mrs. Takata began initiating Reiki Masters. She charged a fee of $10,000 for Mastership even though the training took only one weekend.[27] This high fee was not part of the Usui system, and she may have charged this fee as her way of creating a feeling of respect for Reiki. She said that one should never do treatments or provide training for free, but should always charge a fee or get something in return. She also said that one must study with just one Reiki teacher and stay with that teacher the rest of one's life.[28] In addition, she did not allow her students to take notes or to tape record the classes, and they were not allowed to make any written copies of the Reiki symbols. Everything had to be memorized.[29] It is not certain why she said this or why she taught Reiki this way. What we do know from our research in Japan and the research of others, is that these rules are not part of the way Usui Sensei practiced Reiki. Somehow in the process of bringing Reiki to the West, changes occurred.

Before Mrs. Takata made her transition on December 11, 1980, she had initiated twenty-two Reiki Masters.[30] These twenty-two Masters began teaching others. However, Mrs. Takata had made each one take a sacred oath to teach Reiki exactly as she had taught it. This made it difficult for most of them to change even though some of her rules seemed to go against the nature of Reiki and made it more difficult to learn.

This version of the history of Reiki from Usui Sensei to Mrs. Takata relies on verifiable information that has taken a long time to reach the West. There are a number of reasons for this. After Dr. Hayashi died, Mrs. Takata stated that she was the only Reiki Master in the world.[31] Therefore, most people refrained from researching the history of Reiki, thinking she was the only authority on the subject. Many of the Masters she initiated also discouraged people from doing such research, stating that it was not needed. Add to all this the linguistic, cultural and geographic barriers that separated the United States from Japan and it is easy to see why most authors simply accepted her story as true without seeking verification. Most did not realize that the organization started by Usui Sensei still exists in Japan and that many of his students and the teachers they initiated continue to practice there today.

Reiki Since Mrs. Takata

Reiki energy is very flexible and creative, treating each unique situation with a unique response and working freely with all other forms of healing. The Reiki energy itself provides a wonderful model for the practice of Reiki. This began to be acknowledged gradually after Mrs. Takata passed on. In the mid-1980's, Iris Ishikura, one of Takata's Masters, began charging a more reasonable fee for the Master Level training. The Masters trained by Ishikura at this lower fee began training many other Masters in turn. Out of this group, many were open to change and began allowing the wisdom of the Reiki energy to guide them in the way they should practice and teach Reiki. Because of this, restrictive rules began to fall away. Reiki classes became more open and more supportive of the learning process. Workbooks were created, notes and tape recordings were allowed, reasonable fees were charged and many began studying with more than one teacher. All this generated greater respect for Reiki. It also increased peoples' understanding of Reiki and improved their healing skills. With lower fees, the practice of Reiki began to grow quickly and spread all over the world. There are at least 200,000 Reiki Masters in the world today with well over 1,000,000 practitioners, and the numbers continue to grow!

I learned Reiki I on the Big Island of Hawaii in 1981 from Bethal Phaigh, who had learned from Mrs. Takata. In 1982, I received Reiki II from Bethal. I loved Reiki and started a Reiki practice. Because of the high fee for Reiki Master training and other restrictive rules, I did not think that becoming a Reiki Master was part of my spiritual path. However, Reiki has a way of guiding us in the way we should go, and through a number of coincidences and circumstances I met Diane McCumber in 1989. She was a Reiki Master of the Ishikura lineage and was charging a very reasonable fee to train Reiki Masters. I took her training and began to teach.

I chose to allow the Reiki energy to guide how I would teach. Rather than adhere strictly to the rules set by Mrs. Takata, I wanted to do everything I could to help my students learn Reiki and use it in a way that was right for them. If they wanted to start a Reiki practice or to teach, then I wanted them to be as successful as possible. I took everything I had learned about Reiki to that point, organized the information and placed it in a class workbook that included drawings of the Reiki hand positions. I gave my workbook to students in class. Later I expanded the workbook into a regular book, which evolved into the book you are reading now.

I encouraged students to take notes and to tape record my classes. I also openly answered all questions and actively encouraged all my students to do well. I taught the value of developing one's intuition and having confidence in one's experience and personal decision-making abilities. Knowing that one can always learn more, I continued to study Reiki from others and eventually took the Master Training from three additional Masters. This added tremendously to my understanding of Reiki. Each teacher had gained many unique insights about how Reiki works and how to practice it, and I benefited from their insights.

I make it a point to acknowledge the value of other teachers and practitioners. In my travels, I continue to exchange Reiki information with them, looking for new insights to use myself and pass on to others. Because I based my Reiki practice on an open, adaptive model suggested by the Reiki energy itself, my classes were always full. A newsletter was started that also offered Reiki tapes and other helpful products for those practicing and teaching Reiki. Wanting to maintain high standards for Reiki, I started a teacher certification program (now called our Center Licensed Teachers program) that required additional training and took about a year to complete. Our Licensed Teachers now offer classes across the U.S. and abroad.

ENDNOTES

[1]"Mrs. Takata Speaks, The History of Reiki," 90 minute cassette tape recorded 1979 with transcript, available from Vision Publications, (See Appendix D.)

[2] The Original Reiki Ideals were published in the Fall 1996 issue of the *Reiki News* and are also available at our web site, www.reiki.org. They came from the book *Iyashi No Te (Healing Hands)*, page 227, by Toshitaka Mochizuki, a Japanese Reiki Master, 1995, ISBN 4-88481-420-7 C0011 P1400E.

[3] Inscription on Usui Memorial, Saihoji Temple, Suginami, Tokyo, Japan.

[4] This information comes from Tatsumi-san, one of Dr. Hayashi's last students, who was interviewed by Melissa Riggall in the summer of 1996.

[5] Inscription on Usui Memorial.

[6] "Searching the Roots of Reiki," by Shiomi Takai, published in the magazine *The Twilight Zone*, April 1986, pages 140-143. This article can be viewed on the web at http://www.pwpm.com/threshold/origins2.html. (Note that this Japanese magazine is out of business.)

[7] *Iyashi No Te (Healing Hands)*, by Toshitaka Mochizuki.

[8] Ibid.

[9] *The Twilight Zone*, loc.cit.

[10] Inscription on Usui Memorial.

[11] *Iyashi No Te (Healing Hands)*, by Toshitaka Mochizuki.

[12] Inscription on Usui Memorial.

[13] *Iyashi No Te (Healing Hands)*, by Toshitaka Mochizuki.

[14] *The Twilight Zone*, loc.cit.

[15] *Encyclopedia Britannica*. The 1997 CD-ROM article entitled "Earthquakes Tokyo-Yokohama" contains the following description: "A great earthquake struck the Tokyo-Yokohama metropolitan area near noon on Sept. 1, 1923. The death toll from this shock was estimated at more than 140,000. Fifty-four percent of the brick buildings and 10 percent of the reinforced concrete structures collapsed. Many hundreds of thousands of houses were either shaken down or burned. The shock started a tsunami that reached a height of 12 metres at Atami on Sagami-nada (Sagami Gulf), where it destroyed 155 houses and killed 60 persons."

[16] Inscription on Usui Memorial.

[17] *The Twilight Zone*, loc.cit.

[18] Inscription on Usui Memorial.

[19] According to Toshitaka Mochizuki, in *Iyashi No Te (Healing Hands)*, Taireido was started by Tanaka Monihei, Tenohira-Ryouchi-Kenkyuka, *which* means "The Association for The Study of Palm Treatments," was started by Toshihiro Eguchi, who learned healing from Usui Sensei before founding his own group. Eguchi also wrote books on healing, which are now hard to find. Jintai-Ragium-Gakkai, which means "The Human Body Radium Society," was founded by Matumoto Chiwake, and Shinnoukyou-Honin was a religious group founded by Nishimura Taikan, whose method was called ShinnouKyou-Syokusyu-Shikou Ryoho, meaning "Violet Light Healing Method."

[20] *Dojo, Magic and Exorcism in Modern Japan*, by Winston Davis. Stanford University Press, 1980.

[21] *Reiki Fire*, page 26, by Frank Arjava Petter. Lotus Light: 1997, ISBN 0-914955-50-0.

[22] This list comes from the research of Frank Arjava Petter and Dave King.

[23] Frank Arjava Petter interviewing Tsutomo Oishi, a member of Usui Shiki Reiki Ryoho.

[24] "Mrs. Takata Opens Minds to Reiki," by Vera Graham, *The (San Mateo) Times*, May 17, 1975.

[25] "Mrs. Takata and Reiki Power," by Patsy Matsura, *Honolulu Advertiser*, Feb. 25, 1974.

[26] Mrs. Takata's Reiki certificate, a copy of which can be obtained from the International Center for Reiki Training. Information also taken from Mrs. Takata's handwritten notes dated May 1936.

[27] [28] *Journey into Consciousness*, by Bethal Phaigh, page 130. That Mrs. Takata gave Reiki Master training in a weekend has also been confirmed by other Masters she initiated.

[29] We know that Keizo Ogawa took Reiki Master training from Dr. Mikao Usui and Iichi Taketomi, so it is not likely this rule came from Dr. Usui.

[30] From the tape, "Mrs. Takata Speaks, The History of Reiki." This was also explained to me by Bethal Phaigh in 1981 when I took Reiki I from her.

[31] Takata gave a list of the twenty-two Masters she initiated to her sister before she died. They are: George Araki, Dorothy Baba (deceased), Ursula Baylow, Rick Bockner, Barbara Brown, Fran Brown, Patricia Ewing, Phyllis Lei Furumoto, Beth Gray, John Gray, Iris Ishikura (deceased), Harry Kuboi, Ethel Lombardi, Barbara McCullough, Mary McFadyen, Paul Mitchell, Bethel Phaigh (deceased), Barbara Weber Ray, Shinobu Saito (Takata's sister), Virginia Samdahl, and Wanja Twan.

[32] This is stated on her Reiki flyers dated July 1975 and June 1976. It is also stated in "Mrs. Takata Opens Minds to Reiki," the May 17, 1975 article in *The (San Mateo) Times* based on an interview with Mrs. Takata.

Pictures from Mt. Kurama

Mt. Kurama

Entrance to Kurama Temple

Shrine at San-mon Station honoring Sonten. The deity is Vaisravana. The three symbols on the disks represent power on the left, light in the middle behind the deity and love on the right. The love symbol looks very similar to the mental/emotional symbol of Reiki II

A closer look at the love symbol from Tendai and Kurama-Kokyo Buddhism (see Appendix A, page A-4)

Meditation waterfall

One of three giant cedar trees part way up the mountain

Main Hall

View from Main Hall

Spiral Tiger in front of Main Hall

Ritual Bell

Roots on the path near the top of the mountain

Okunoin Mao-den Shrine at the top of Mt. Kurama

Looking out from Okunoin Mao-den

Saihoji Temple in Tokyo where the Usui Memorial is located

Chapter 3
The International Center for Reiki Training

In 1988 I founded the Center for Spiritual Development. In 1991 the name was changed to the Center for Reiki Training as Reiki became our only focus. In 1997, because of all the classes that were being taught abroad, "International" was added to our name.

The Reiki training offered by the International Center for Reiki Training is based on the original Usui system of Reiki. However, the Center has also added innovations that have been proven to increase Reiki's effectiveness as a healing art. These include scanning, beaming, meditation, a technique called aura clearing that removes negative psychic energy, healing attunements and acknowledgment of the role played by spiritual beings in the healing process. While most of these are part of Advanced Reiki Training (ART) and Master Training, scanning and beaming are covered in Part II of this book, and brief descriptions of scanning, beaming, aura clearing and healing attunements are included below.

The attunement process used by the Center in all Reiki Level I, II, ART and Master classes is a combination of the Usui system and a special Tibetan technique. In the Reiki III/Master class, the Usui/Tibetan method of giving attunements is taught along with the original Usui system of attunements. Students wishing to practice the original Usui system of Reiki can easily do so as all additions to the Usui system are clearly explained in class.

Additions the Center has made to the original Usui system came because of inner guidance and our desire to provide greater value. They were added only after they had been thoroughly tested and were proven to enhance healing. The following techniques are ones I developed at the Center.

Scanning and Beaming

Scanning is a way of finding those places in yourself or others which are most in need of healing, then administering Reiki to them. Beaming is a way to focus Reiki energy either on the aura or on specific areas of the body. Chapter 9 explains scanning and beaming in detail.

Aura Clearing

The presence of negative psychic energy in the body or the aura is the cause of most illness and dysfunction. We therefore developed aura clearing, a Reiki technique for removing negative psychic energy. Formerly called Reiki psychic surgery, this highly effective process uses Reiki energy to empower the hands so that practitioners can grasp negative psychic energy within or around themselves or others and send it up to the light. The positive results of this process in healing and well-being are immediately apparent. Reiki aura clearing is taught in Advanced Reiki Training. (See Appendix C.)

Healing Attunement

A special healing attunement also has been developed.The healing attunement uses the same high-frequency energies used in the initiations, but only for healing.This process opens a spiritual door through which powerful, higher-frequency Reiki energies are able to flow and through which the Reiki guides can work more effectively. Because the healing attunements do not initiate a person into Reiki, they can be given to anyone and are especially useful prior to a regular Reiki treatment. The healing attunement process is taught in the Reiki III/Master class. (See Appendix C.)

Three-Step Treatment

A three-step treatment is recommended for those who have taken ART/III Master training. The healing attunement is given first, followed by aura clearing and then a regular Reiki treatment using all the hand positions. This is a powerful combination that speeds up the healing process so that fewer treatments are needed and deeper healing takes place.

Becoming a Reiki Master/Teacher

The Center actively encourages and supports students to become Reiki Masters and teachers if they feel guided to do so. After taking Reiki I & II and taking time to practice and gain experience, individuals can go on to take ART/III Master training. They can then begin teaching on their own as independent Reiki Masters or choose to become licensed by the Center to teach Reiki. (See Appendix C for more information on training and certification available through the Center.)

Many take the Master training who do not intend to teach but rather to use the increased healing energies, symbols and skills for their own healing, to help friends and family and to improve their healing practice.

Karuna Reiki®

Karuna Reiki® training is an advanced training course offered only to Reiki Masters. It strengthens their healing energy, allowing it to work more deeply and produce beneficial results more quickly. Eight healing symbols and four master symbols are taught in two levels. Each symbol has a distinctive purpose and vibration. These additional healing tools help one to be a more effective healer. Karuna Reiki® is the next step beyond the Reiki Master level. (See Appendix C for more details.)

The Center Licensed Teachers Program

The Center Licensed Teachers program is an advanced curriculum of study that takes at least one year to complete. Students must take all our classes; Reiki I & II, Advanced Reiki Training, Reiki III/Master, and Karuna Reiki® Master, review each class, take a written examination, write a paper and document a minimum of 100 complete Reiki treatments. Then they co-teach each class before teaching it on their own.

To maintain their license, teachers must review classes once a year and turn in class reviews from each student taught. They agree to support the Center Philosophy and Purpose, the Original Reiki Ideals, and to work on their own personal healing. They also agree to abide by a code of ethics and to teach the required subjects for each class. As long as those subjects are covered in class, teachers are free to add meditations or other healing techniques they have found to be useful.

These high standards allow our Licensed Teachers to provide quality Reiki training that is consistent and verifiable. They have also helped us become qualified to offer Continuing Education Units (CEU's) to nurses, massage therapists and athletic trainers who take our classes. In addition, our high standards provide the basis for our plans to work in hospitals and doctors' offices and otherwise interface with the medical community. (See my article Reiki in Hospitals in Appendix B) If you are interested in participating in our Center Licensed Teachers program, please contact us and order one of our Center Licensed Teachers booklets. (See Appendix C.)

The Center Philosophy

- Honesty and clarity in one's thinking.
- Willingness to recognize prejudice in oneself and replace it with truth and love. Compassion for those who have decided not to do this.
- Speaking the truth without judgment or blame.
- Respecting others' right to form their own values and beliefs.
- Placing greater value on learning from experience and inner guidance than on the teachings of an outside authority.
- Basing the value of a theory or technique on the verifiable results it helps one achieve.
- Being open to results rather than attached to them.
- Taking personal responsibility for one's situation in life.
- Assuming that one has the resources to solve any problem encountered, or the ability to develop them.
- Using negative and positive experiences to heal and to grow.
- Trusting completely in the Higher Power regardless of the name one chooses to call it.
- Complete expression of Love as the highest goal.

The Center Purpose

- To establish and maintain standards for teaching Reiki.
- To train and license Reiki teachers.
- To create instructional manuals for use in Reiki classes.
- To encourage the establishment of Reiki support groups where people can give and receive Reiki treatments.
- To help people develop and use their Reiki skills.
- To encourage students to become successful Reiki teachers if they are guided to do so.
- To research new information about Reiki and to develop new techniques to improve its use.
- To openly acknowledge the value provided by all Reiki people regardless of their lineage or affiliation.
- To promote friendly cooperation among all Reiki practitioners and teachers toward the goal of healing ourselves and Planet Earth through the use of Reiki.

All Reiki Groups Have Value

We affirm that all Reiki practitioners and teachers are being guided by Reiki energy to practice and teach Reiki in a way that is exactly right for them. We also affirm that all Reiki practitioners and groups are working to heal themselves, each other and the planet. Because of this, we honor and respect all Reiki practitioners, teachers and groups regardless of lineage or organizational affiliation.

We have focused on making our system of Reiki the best we can based on our inner guidance and our experience. We also affirm that Reiki students are capable of deciding for themselves which system or teacher is right for them. We encourage all Reiki students to study with more than one teacher or system if they are guided to do so.

Love grants in a moment what toil can hardly achieve in an age.

Johann Wolfgang Goethe

Part II

Elements of Reiki Treatment

Chapter 4
Using Reiki

Reiki is a very easy healing technique to use. After receiving the Reiki attunement, all that is necessary to start Reiki flowing is to request it to do so. Just ask or intend that it begin to flow and it will. This can be done simply by saying the word "Reiki" to yourself at the beginning of a healing session. Reiki is always ready to flow and it will do so whenever you want it to. Simply placing your hands on someone with the intention of giving a treatment will be enough to start it flowing. It is not necessary to meditate or concentrate or go into an altered state to use Reiki. Reiki flows so easily that just thinking or talking about it turns it on. In fact, as I write this section of the manual I feel my Reiki flowing simply because I am thinking about it.

One thing that sometimes happens, especially in groups, is that the people giving Reiki will start talking. This tends to focus attention away from the client and can also decrease the value of the treatment. Although Reiki will flow when you are talking, it works much better when you are in a meditative state, allowing your consciousness to merge with the Reiki energy.

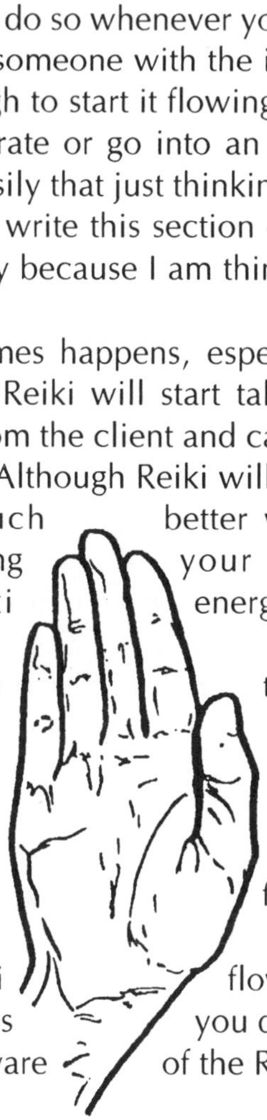

When giving a Reiki treatment, it is important to keep your fingers together. This will concentrate the energy and create a stronger flow. Be aware of the sensations in your hands such as warmth, tingling, vibrations, pulsations or a flow of energy.

You may also feel Reiki flowing through other parts of your body. As you dwell on Reiki, your mind will begin to be aware of the Reiki consciousness.

You may experience this as feelings of relaxation, joy, love, well-being, security, upliftment, unlimited potential, freedom, creativity, beauty, balance, harmony, and other positive states. Allow these feelings to become your feelings. If other thoughts come up, gently brush them away and bring your attention back to the consciousness of Reiki. As you do this, not only will you be allowing Reiki to flow more strongly, you will also be receiving a deep healing yourself.

By meditating on the consciousness of Reiki, you will also be entering a state of mind that allows your Reiki guides to work more closely with you. They will be better able to channel their Reiki through you as well as send it directly to the client.

The most important way to increase the effectiveness of Reiki is to come from love, compassion, and kindness. This will create a feeling of emotional safety for clients, encouraging them to more fully accept the Reiki energy. It will also open the doors to your healing potential, increasing the strength of your Reiki, and providing a deeper healing for you!

Another interesting effect is that Reiki sometimes flows out the bottom of your feet. If you feel this happening, feel free to use your feet to give Reiki too. By standing close to the client, the Reiki that flows from them will treat the client's aura before entering the body where it is needed, or it may simply travel up the outside of your legs and be added to the Reiki coming from your hands.

The question sometimes comes up as to the minimum and maximum amount of time that Reiki should be given. Since Reiki is guided by God, it can never cause harm. You can never give too little or too much Reiki. If all you have is a few minutes to give Reiki, go ahead. Reiki will always help. You never can tell how much good even a short treatment will provide. While specific results cannot be guaranteed, short treatments of a few minutes or less have relieved headaches and toothaches, healed bee stings, stopped bleeding, and even set and mended broken bones along with many other valuable results. On the other hand, treatments of several hours or longer will only improve the value of Reiki. You will not overcharge the client with energy or cause any harm whatsoever by giving long treatments.

Reiki will not only treat the area where you place your hands but will often travel to other areas of the body where it is needed. For example, when the hands are placed on the head, Reiki will treat the head but may also travel to the stomach. Conversely, when the hands are placed on the stomach, Reiki will treat this area but could also travel to the neck. Treating the feet can also result in Reiki flowing to the back.

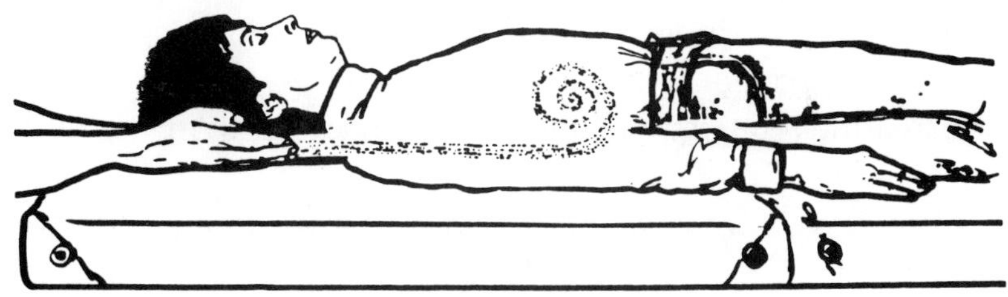

Intuition can play an important role when treating specific symptoms. First try placing your hands over the area of concern. If you feel a lot of Reiki flowing, then stay there. If Reiki does not flow well, ask what the client is feeling. If neither of you feel Reiki is treating the area of concern, ask your intuition to show you the best place to treat the condition and move your hands wherever you are directed. If you feel more Reiki flowing there and the client reports the symptoms subsiding, then you know you received the guidance correctly. Often, the best place to treat a condition is not where the symptoms are manifesting. Always ask to be guided to the best place to treat the condition. You can use the scanning technique mentioned in Chapter 9, or simply ask to be guided to the right place. Trust in your inner guidance even if you think it is illogical or wrong or just the product of your imagination.

The hand positions for treating oneself and others illustrated in Chapters 6-8 are meant as a general guide only. You do not need to strictly adhere to them. Use your intuition. If you feel guided to leave out a position or to add a new one, go ahead. A good rule of thumb is to stay in each position a minimum of three minutes to allow time for Reiki to start flowing. If it flows strongly, then in the context of a standard ninety-minute treatment, stay a maximum of ten minutes and move on. If you were to stay longer, you might not have time to give a complete treatment unless you intended to go longer than 1½ hours.

> *There is a light in this world . . . a healing spirit much stronger than any darkness we may encounter. We sometimes lose sight of this force . . . where there is suffering, too much pain. And suddenly the spirit will emerge . . . through lives of ordinary people, and answer in extraordinary ways. God speaks in the silence of the heart and we listen.*
>
> *Mother Teresa*

Chapter 5
The Reiki Symbols

There are no symbols in First Degree Reiki and they are not necessary to give a Reiki treatment. However, the symbols that are given in Second Degree Reiki and beyond, and the attunements that empower them, add to the strength and versatility of the system of Reiki healing.

Reiki symbols are sacred. It is part of the Reiki tradition that they be kept confidential. They are only revealed to those who have taken Second Degree Reiki or higher and received the attunement that empowers them. The reason for the secrecy is two-fold. First there is a personal issue. By keeping the symbols secret, you demonstrate your respect for them. If others reveal the symbols or display them in print, as several authors have chosen to do, this cannot affect your own personal relationship with the symbols. As long as you keep them secret, you yourself are demonstrating respect.

The second reason for keeping the symbols secret prior to the attunement is consideration for others. Since the power of the symbols comes from the attunement, showing them to those who have not received the attunement will not help them and could cause confusion. However, their nature and purpose can be discussed without violating this trust.

Some Usui Reiki symbols are made from Japanese kanji characters; they are simply words from the Japanese language whose translations can be found in any Japanese/English dictionary. The distant healing and master symbols, for example, are made completely from Japanese characters, both in their names and in the way they are drawn. But the origin of the first two Reiki symbols is more complex. While the names of the power and mental/emotional symbols are Japanese, the symbols themselves may be derived from shamanic sources or may be a combination of Sanskrit and kanji figures. In fact, our trip to Japan revealed that the mental/emotional symbol likely came from the Sanskrit seed syllable *hrih* which the Tendai Buddhists call the love or harmony symbol. (See Appendix A)

It is interesting to note that the attunement actually empowers the symbols so that they will fulfill their intended purpose; without the attunement, the symbols do not seem to do much. This has been verified many times. Students are given the symbols to memorize before the attunement process takes place. Many are psychic and some are healers who are able to see and feel the Reiki energies. All report similar effects. Before the attunement the symbols don't seem to have an influence on the Reiki energies. After the attunement, the effect is definitely there.

Reiki symbols are transcendental. Rather than affecting only the subconscious mind as most symbols do, the Reiki symbols connect directly to the God-Consciousness. Whenever a Reiki symbol is used by someone who has Second Degree Reiki, the Rei or God-Consciousness responds by changing the way the Reiki energy functions. This process operates under a divine covenant or sacred agreement between God and those who have Second Degree Reiki. A person does not have to be in an altered state for the symbols to work. They work automatically, every time they are used.

Reiki symbols are like keys that open doors to higher levels of awareness/manifestation. They can also be thought of as buttons; whenever you "push" one, you automatically get specific results.

Of course, the symbols must be used correctly to activate them. However, this does not mean that there is only one correct way for everyone to draw them. The symbols were never meant to be exact and variations do exist between teachers. Even Mrs. Takata didn't draw the symbols the same way each time. There are also some slight differences between the symbols of the original twenty-two Masters she taught. Apparently she was guided to make minor variations in the symbols for each student depending on the vibration of the moment and what each student needed.

When a Reiki Master shows the Reiki symbols to a student and gives the attunement for them, an imprinting takes place that links the image the student has been shown to the metaphysical energies the symbol represents. This is based on the stimulus/response mechanism in the brain. Whenever a specific stimulus repeatedly accompanies a particular experience, a relationship develops between the stimulus and a person's response to it. This was demonstrated by Pavlov in his famous experiment. Whenever he fed his dog, he rang a bell. After doing this over and over, all he had to do was ring the bell and the dog salivated. Because the energies of the Reiki attunement are of a transcendental nature (and because people hopefully learn more quickly than dogs!), this process is speeded up so that a person needs to be exposed to the symbols only briefly. During the attunement, the energy the symbol represents comes down and links itself to the symbol. Then, whenever the student thinks of the symbol, the energy the symbol represents automatically begins to flow.

Because Mrs. Takata did not allow her students to make copies of the symbols, they had to memorize them. Many did not have perfect memories and when the symbols were passed on from teacher to student over and over again, with no one being allowed to write them down, many variations developed.

We now find that the symbols used by some Reiki teachers look nothing like the original symbols used by Dr. Usui, yet they work just the same. Therefore, the correct way for students to draw the symbols is the way they were shown by their Reiki Master at the time they received the attunement for them. In spite of any outward differences in appearance, each student's symbols still work.

The power of the symbols is not in their outward appearance but in the attunement energies that become attached to them. Even so, many students still want to know what Dr. Usui's symbols really looked like. We have received many requests from Reiki students for copies of the Usui Reiki symbols and I describe how to get a copy at the end of Appendix D.

The following descriptions explain a number of proven uses for the symbols. However, Reiki symbols have their own energy or consciousness, and it is possible to meditate on them and be shown how to use them directly from the God-Consciousness that is inherent in the symbols themselves. Practice the following, but also feel free to experiment with the symbols and you will discover many more uses.

Activating Reiki Symbols

There are many ways to activate Reiki symbols. You can draw them in the air in front of you or on or near the client. The symbols can be drawn using your fire finger which is the one next to the index finger, or you can imagine a beam of light coming out of the palm chakra and draw them by moving the flattened hand in the air. You can also activate a symbol by thinking of its name, or by saying it out loud if no one is around or if you are only with persons who have had Reiki II or higher. You can also visualize the symbol or imagine yourself drawing it. Any of these ways will activate Reiki symbols. The important thing is your intention: intend to activate the symbol and it will activate. The above methods are simply ways of expressing your intention.

The Power Symbol

The name of the power symbol means "put all the power of the universe here." The power symbol is used to increase the power of Reiki or to focus Reiki on a specific location. Anytime you want to increase the strength of the Reiki treatment you are giving, just think of the name or visualize the symbol and your Reiki will get stronger! It can also be used to seal the space around the client and prevent the healing energies from leaking away. This can be seen psychically and appears at times as a box of white light or at other times as a sphere of golden light surrounding the client. The power symbol can be used anytime while giving a treatment but is especially effective if used at the beginning to increase the power and at the end to seal in the healing energies. The power symbol can be used to clear a room of negative psychic energy and seal it in light, making it a sacred space. It can be used to protect yourself, your loved ones, your car, your home, or anything you value. Because Reiki works on all levels, the protection it provides is also on all levels and includes protection from physical harm, as well as protection from verbal and emotional confrontations and from psychic attack. You can also use the power symbol to bless others; just think of its name as you shake hands or hug someone you want to bless. Experiment and you will find many other uses.

The Mental/Emotional Symbol

The name of this symbol means "God and humanity become one." This symbol is used in emotional and mental healing. It balances the right and left sides of the brain, bringing harmony and peace. It is especially useful for healing relationship problems. It can be used with any sort of mental/emotional distress such as nervousness, fear, depression, anger, sadness, etc. Psychically, the energy of this symbol sometimes takes the form of a bubble coming out of the heart chakra of the practitioner for emotional healing or out of the solar plexus chakra for mental healing. Sometimes these two energies work together and mix in front of the practitioner before surrounding and/or entering the client. This symbol can be used to heal addictions as well as problems with weight loss or smoking. It can be used to improve memory and is especially useful at those odd moments when one loses the car keys or forgets a person's name. It can be used to enhance the use of affirmations, causing them to enter more deeply into the subconscious mind. It is also wonderful for studying, learning or taking tests.

Healing Unwanted Habits:
Weight Loss, Cigarettes, Alcohol, Drugs, etc.

The mental/emotional symbol can be used to change or eliminate unwanted habits. Write your name on a piece of paper along with the unwanted habit and the mental/emotional healing symbol. Then hold the paper between your hands treating it with Reiki. This will send Reiki to the parts of your mind and emotions that relate to the unwanted habit, and will begin healing them. Do this for twenty minutes or longer each day. Carry the paper with you. If you feel the unwanted compulsion come up during the day, take out the paper and Reiki it.

Example: If you want to lose weight, write your name on the paper, the word "Food" and the mental/emotional healing symbol. Reiki the paper each day, and also before each meal.

You will find it much easier to eat less, and to eat only healthy foods. You could also use the words "healthy weight loss" on the paper or create another appropriate phrase yourself.

The Distant Healing Symbol

The name of this symbol means "May the Buddha in me connect to the Buddha in you to promote harmony and peace." It works on the basis of the unity of all life - the reality that the same divine consciousness or "Buddha nature" is in us all. This symbol is used to send Reiki to others at a distance. You can send Reiki to people across the room, across town, or even in other parts of the country or the world. Distance is no barrier when using this symbol. Sometimes a picture of the client is used in conjunction with the symbol.

I have often used this distant healing symbol with my clients who are coming for a Reiki session. By sending Reiki to them while they are on their way to the appointment, I find they always arrive calm and relaxed. I have also used Reiki for past-life regression, hypnosis and guided meditation. By using the distant healing symbol with the mental/emotional healing symbol, I am able to send Reiki to them during the session from across the room to help facilitate the healing process.

This sometimes has interesting effects. Without my telling them what I am doing, the Reiki energy will often blend with the person's inner imagery and actually become part of the scenario they are experiencing. Having its own wisdom, the Reiki energy knows exactly how to do this. Sometimes they see it surrounding them in the form of a protective white mist. It has also worked to empower them by flowing through them and out of their hands, which they then direct spontaneously toward the area of difficulty to help solve the problem.

The distant symbol can also be used to bridge time. You can use it to send Reiki into the future. If you know you will be involved in an important activity in the future, and you know the date and time of the event, you can send Reiki to the event so that it will be there to help you when the time comes. When it is used in this way, the Reiki energy stores up like a battery. When the time comes, its healing energy descends to surround you and help you. People have used this technique to help them with job interviews, tests, trips to the dentist, surgery or other important events.

This symbol can also be used to send Reiki into the past. If you had a traumatic experience in the past and you know the approximate date, you can use the distant symbol to send Reiki back to heal the trauma. It often helps if you have a picture of yourself close to the time the trauma occurred. If you don't know the date and don't have a picture, it will still work simply by naming the problem and asking that Reiki go to the cause and heal it. This technique can also be used to heal problems that stem from past lives.

The distant symbol can be used like a homing device. If you don't know the area of the body to treat for a particular condition, or where the cause of a problem is, just use the distant symbol, asking it to send the Reiki energy to the cause of the problem, and Reiki will go there without you needing to know where or what the cause is.

The distant symbols can also be used for exorcism and spirit release work. This is a simple process that is very powerful. It is not based on a contest between you and the spirit, therefore it does not drain your energy or place you in harm's way. Just use the distant symbols to send Reiki to the spirit, then call on the Ascended Masters and ask them to take the spirit up into the light. Continue sending Reiki for several more minutes or until you feel the process is complete. The Ascended Masters will do all the work and deal with the spirit in exactly the right way to create a healing for both the person and the spirit.

Using the Distant Healing Symbol

Sending distant Reiki is a two-step process. First, establish the connection by using the distant symbol with the person's name or picture. Then send Reiki. Reiki will begin going to the person and continue as long as you intend to send Reiki. Here are several ways to send distant Reiki:

- Use a picture of the person. Place the picture in front of you and draw the distant symbol in the air, imagining you are drawing it over the picture. Then beam Reiki toward the picture and it will go to that person.

- Do the above, only hold the picture between your hands and request Reiki to flow to the person.

- Write the person's name on a piece of paper, draw the distant healing symbol and hold the paper between your hands.

- Simply hold your hands up in the direction in which you imagine the person to be, draw the distant healing symbol and beam Reiki to them.

- Use a teddy bear as a stand-in or surrogate for the person. Say the person's name three times, then draw the distant healing symbol down the front of the teddy bear's body. Then do a standard treatment using all the hand positions on the teddy bear intending the treatment to go to the person. It is also possible to do scanning and beaming with the teddy bear. If you do not have a teddy bear, you may use a pillow instead.

- While driving, intend that the steering wheel represents the person you want to send Reiki to. Think of the distant symbol or say its name, then say the name of the person you want to send Reiki to. Reiki will flow to the person while you are driving and have both hands on the wheel!

- Experiment sending Reiki to Jesus, Buddha, God, the full moon, the earth, pagan gods, your spirit guides, angels, etc. People who have done this type of distant healing report receiving tremendous healing back from these high spiritual beings. Doing this also creates a strong connection so that your prayers to them are empowered.

- Use the distant healing symbol to send Reiki to people you knew in the past or to people on TV or in the newspapers, especially those who are injured or otherwise in need of help.

- Send Reiki to national or world crisis situations using one of the above techniques.

While it is best to send distant Reiki only to those who have requested it, as they will be the most receptive, there may be times when you will want to help someone who is not aware that you could help them or for whom requesting help may be difficult. People in comas can't request help, but still might want it if they knew about the possibility. Also, you may want to send Reiki to heal the earth or to a crisis situation. In these cases, just say a prayer asking for permission to send Reiki. You may get permission or you may not, but it is important to follow your inner guidance. Remember, Reiki can do no harm. Also, Reiki respects a person's free will. If you send Reiki to someone who does not want it, the Reiki will not affect them.

Group Distant Healing

Distant healing can be sent by a group of Reiki II practitioners with powerful results. Just sit in a circle and place the name or picture of the person in the middle. Have everyone draw the distant symbol and say its name three times, then say the person's name three times, then beam Reiki to the picture or name in the center. Remember, Reiki works by intention. Just use your imagination to think of other ways to use it.

Empowering Goals

If you have been blocked in the achievement of a particular goal, it usually means there is something that needs to heal before you will be able to achieve that goal. In addition, the achievement of any goal will be easier if all its aspects are surrounded with the loving, harmony-producing energy of Reiki.

Write your name on a piece of paper or a 3 x 5 card. Write down a name for your goal, or just a description of it. If dates are involved, write them down too. Then draw all three symbols on the paper or card. Reiki it for twenty minutes or more each day. Carry the card or paper with you wherever you go. Give it Reiki whenever you have a spare moment. Continue to actively work to achieve your goal. You will find everything working much better. If the goal is in harmony with your higher good, you will achieve it!

Reiki is a powerful healing energy that has many possibilities for the innovative practitioner. It is exciting that something as valuable as Reiki is now becoming widely available.

If we are to solve the personal and global problems that face us, it is important to make effective use of the healing resources available to us and to be thankful for the techniques that are now surfacing from ancient knowledge. These are the most interesting of times, filled with the possibility of important discoveries, the development of higher consciousness and the transformation of society. Let us take charge of our lives and create an exciting adventure out of the challenges we face!

Chapter 6
Hand Positions for Self-Treatment

This Chapter and Chapter 8 present the standard hand positions for Reiki treatment. The next chapter illustrates another effective method, which is to treat the aura using hand positions several inches away from the body. You can use either method, or both.

In some areas of the country, only licensed medical doctors or nurses or massage therapists may legally touch a client's body. If this is the case and you don't have such a license, use the treatment method shown in Chapter 7.

Position #1

Place your hands over your face with the fingers at the top of the forehead and the hands touching.

Position #2A

Place your hands on top of your head with the fingers touching but not overlapping. Palms are close to the top of the ears.

Position #2B

This is an alternate position for #2A. Place your hands on the sides of your head over the ears.

Position #3

Place your hands on the back of your head with the base of the palms at the base of the skull.

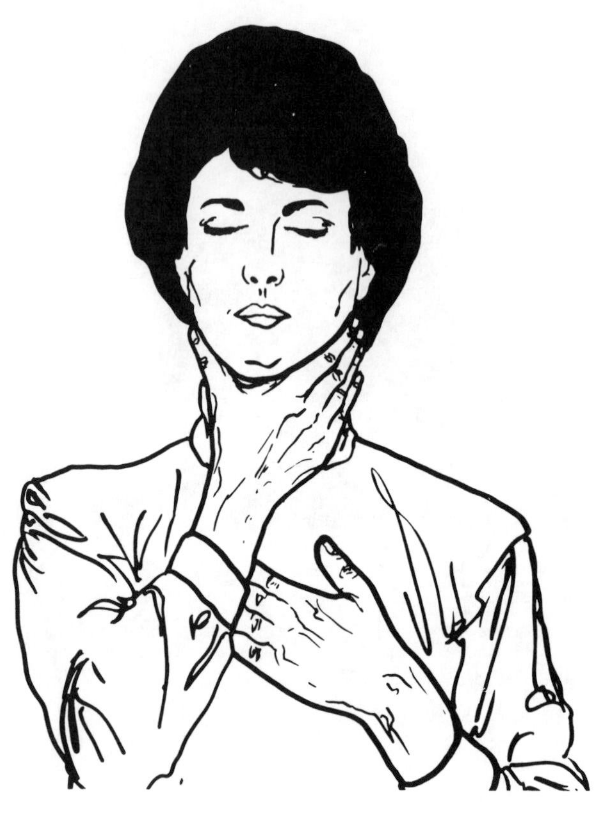

Position #4

Place the right hand over your throat and the left hand over your heart.

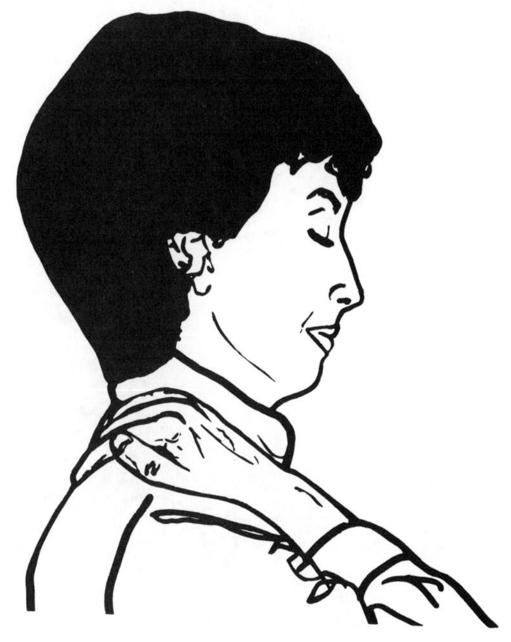

Position #5

Place both hands over your shoulders close to the neck.

Position #6

Place your hands with the fingers touching over the upper stomach just below the rib cage.

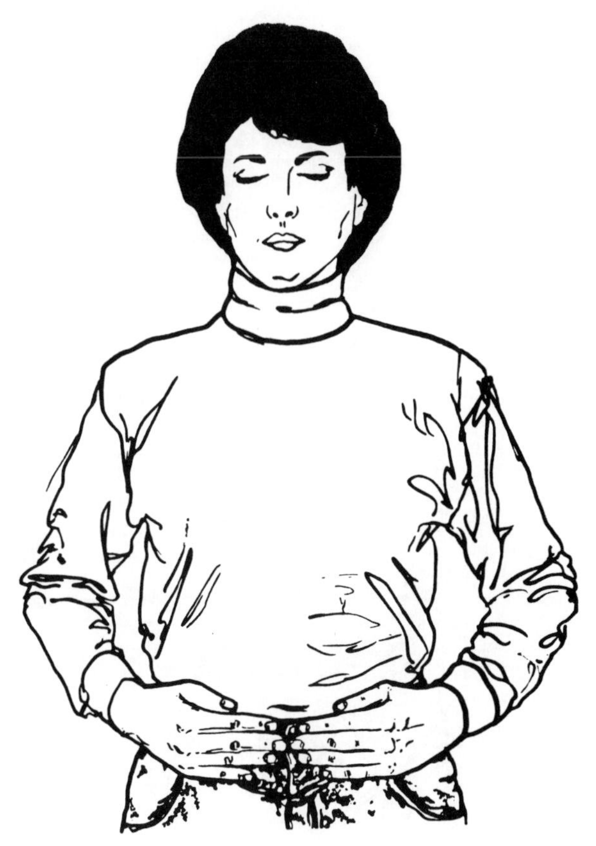

Position #7

Place your hands over the middle stomach with the fingers touching at the navel.

Position #8

Place your hands on the lower stomach with the base of the hands near or on the hip bones and the fingertips over the pubic bone.

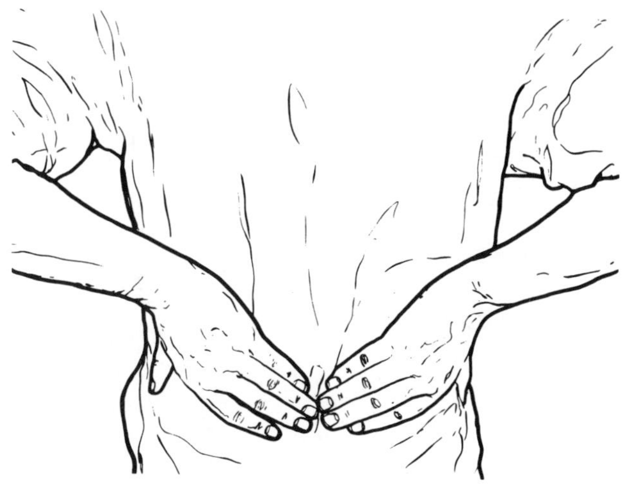

Position #9

Place your hands on the middle back with the fingers touching.

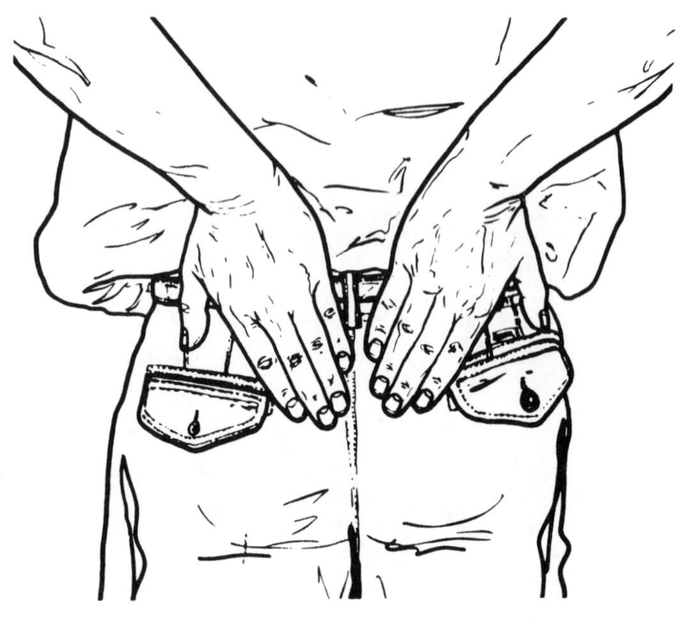

Position #10

Place your hands on the lower back with the finger tips over the sacrum.

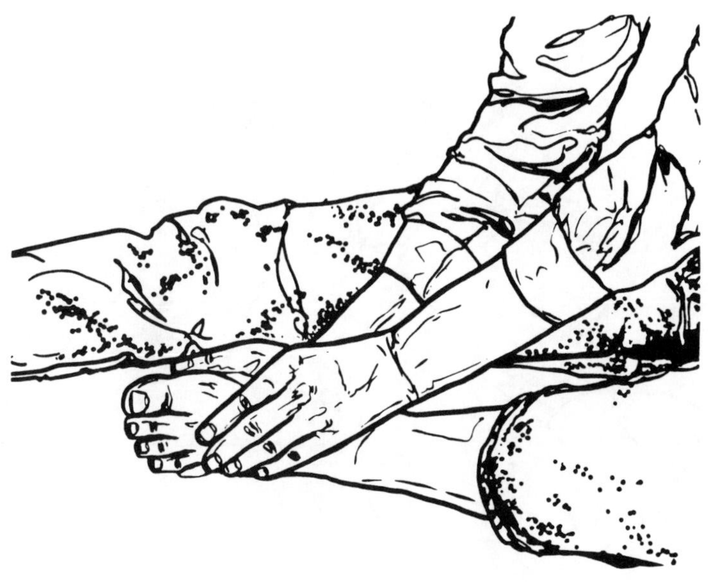

Position #11

Hold your left foot with both hands in a way that is comfortable.

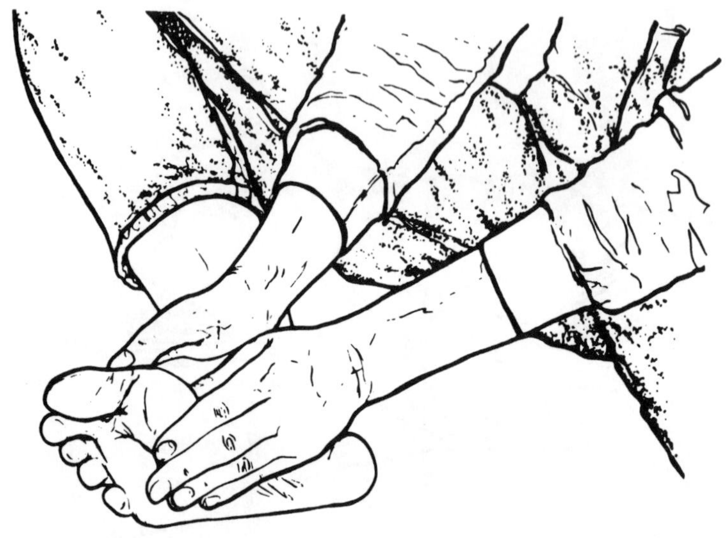

Position #12

Hold your right foot with both hands in a way that is comfortable.

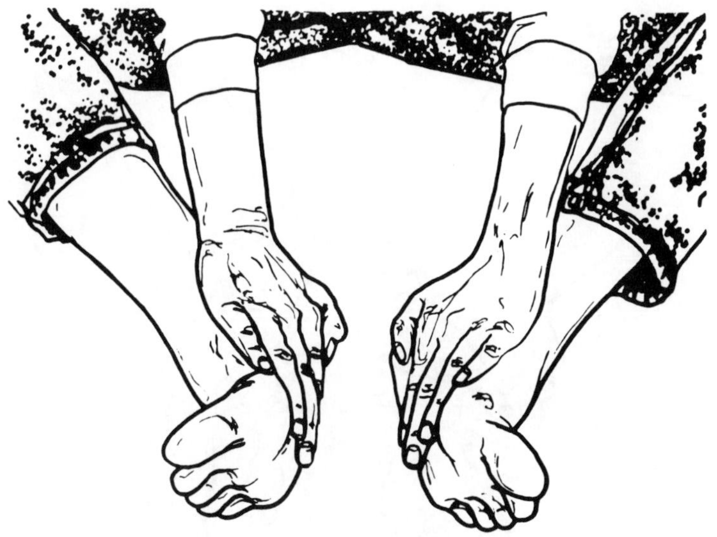

Position #13A

Hold your right foot with the right hand and your left foot with the left hand in a way that is comfortable.

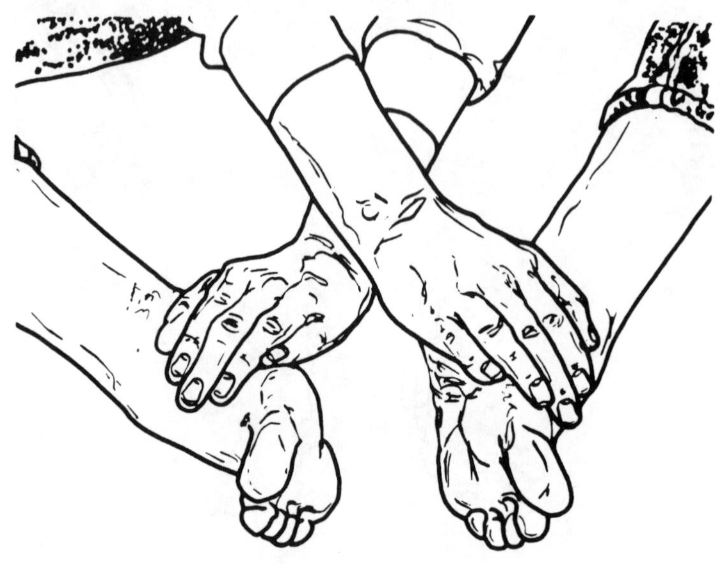

Position #13B

Hold your right foot with the left hand and your left foot with the right hand in a way that is comfortable.

Chapter 7
Alternate Treatment for Self or Others

A complete treatment can be given to yourself or others with the hands one to four inches from the body using the standard hand positions. Because the hands are in the aura, Reiki will treat the aura before it enters the physical body. Illness exists first in the aura before manifesting in the physical body. Treating through the aura will help prevent physical illness.

The Reiki energies act in a different, often more powerful way with this technique. They easily travel through the aura to other parts of the energy field, often flowing through and surrounding several areas at once, filling them with warm, loving, nurturing energy before entering the physical body just where they are needed.

Many people find this method to be more effective, while others prefer physical contact. You can use one or the other, or you can mix the two. Simply allow your intuition to guide you in deciding where to use physical contact and where to treat through the aura.

In some areas of the country, you must be a licensed nurse or doctor or massage therapist in order to legally touch the physical body. Unless you are, it would be better to treat through the aura and avoid hands-on positions. Also, some people do not like to be touched and others suffer from burns or other conditions that are painful to the touch. In such cases, do the complete treatment without touching.

Use this position to beam Reiki to your head, neck, and shoulders. You can direct the beam by changing the angle of your hands. In addition to healing your upper body, it will also fill the upper aura with vibrant, healing colors - very powerful!

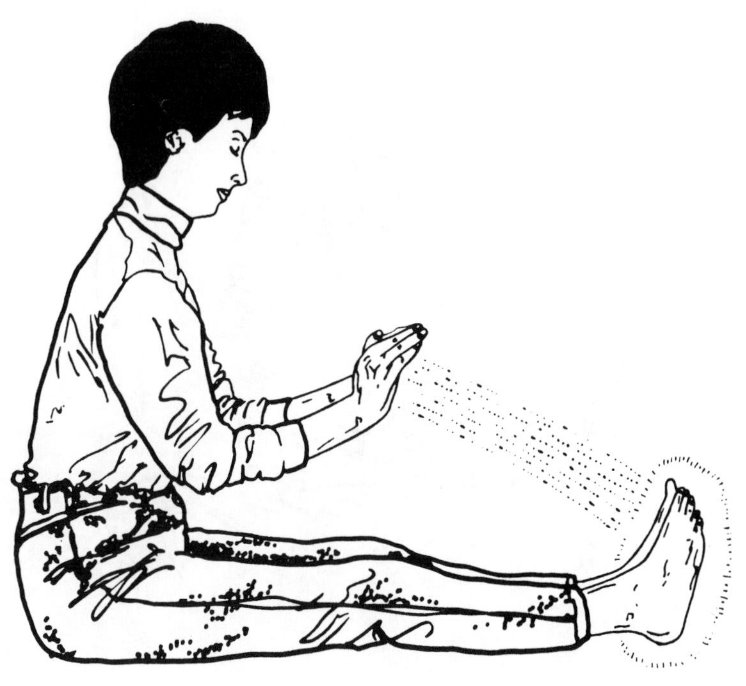

If holding your feet is difficult, beam Reiki to them.

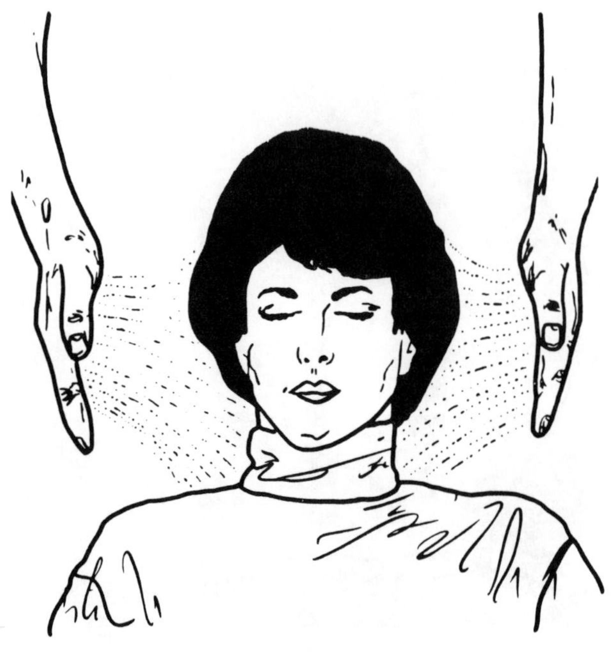

This is similar to position #2A, page II-41. Try the other positions and notice the difference.

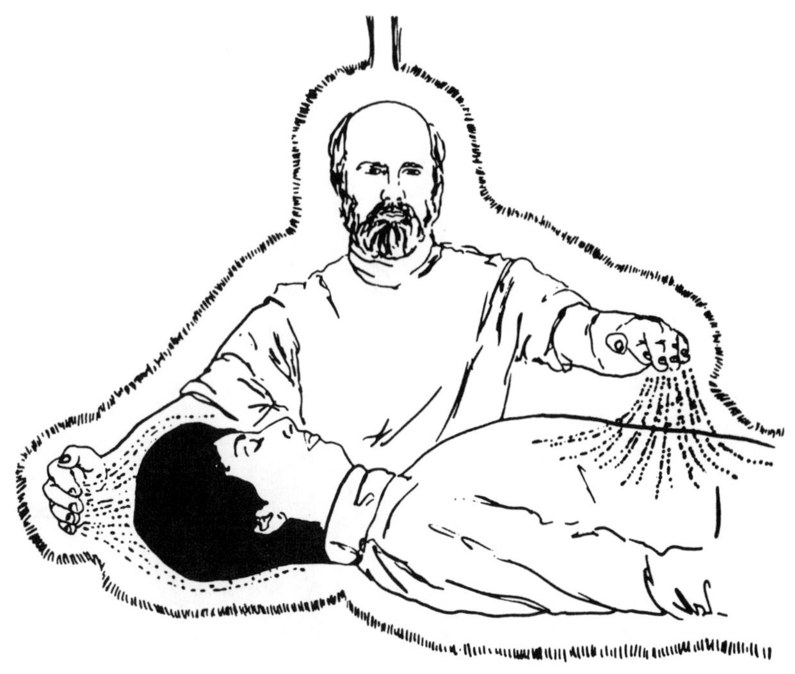

This position is used to heal the connection between the Crown and Solar Plexus chakras.

Chapter 8
Hand Positions for Treating Others

The hand positions illustrated in this chapter can be used in place of, or in conjunction with, the aura treatments shown in the previous chapter.

Again, you may need to avoid touching clients in cases like these:

- If the law allows only licensed nurses, doctors or massage therapists to touch clients and you don't have a license of that kind.

- If your client does not like to be touched.

- If your client has burns or any other condition that is painful to the touch.

In all such cases, treat the client through the aura rather than using the hands-on method.

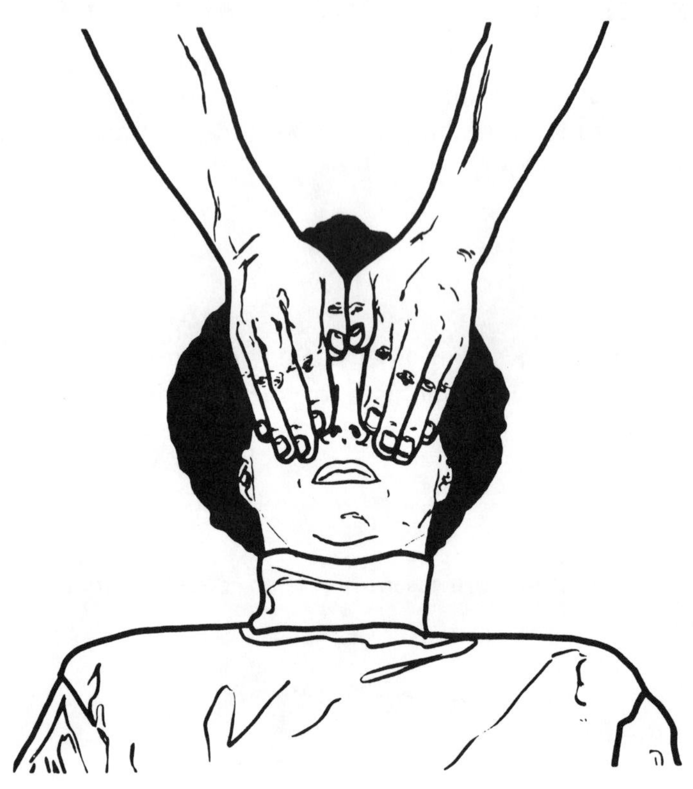

Position #1

Hands are together with thumbs touching. Carefully curve your hands so that the palms do not touch the eyes or eyelashes. Slowly place the base of the hands on top of the forehead with the fingers gently resting on the cheeks. If your hands sweat, place a tissue over the eyes.

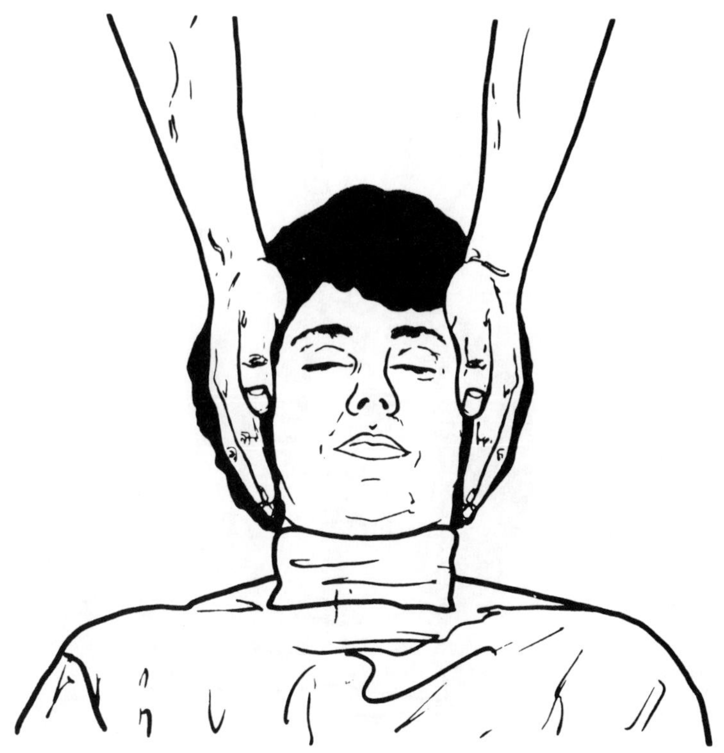

Position #2A

Place your hands on each side of the head cupped over the ears with the fingers pointing toward the feet.

Position #2B

This position can be used in addition to or instead of position #2A. Let your intuition guide you. Place the base of your hands together and rest them on the crown of the head with fingers extending toward the ears.

Position #3

Gently cradle the head in your hands. The hands are touching and the fingers are at the base of the skull.

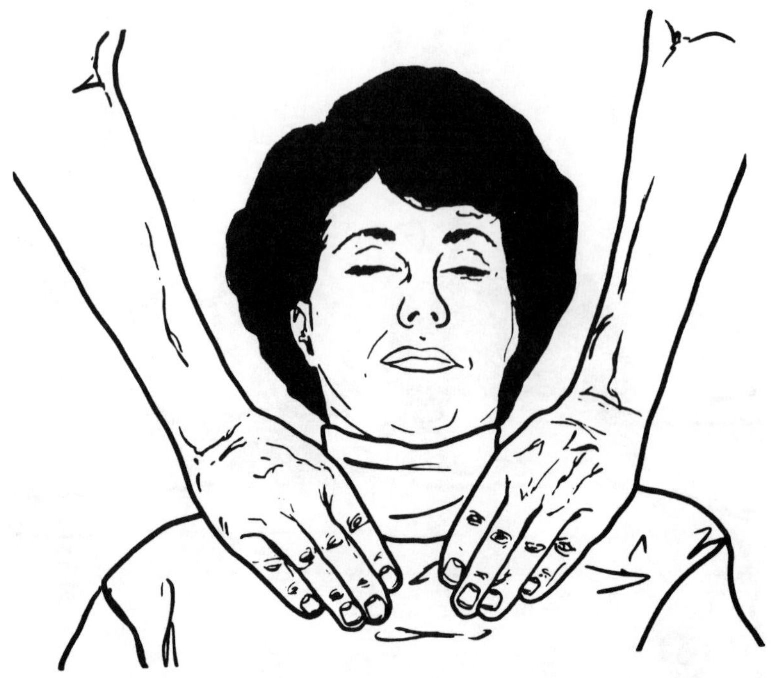

Position #4A

Place your hands over the collarbone with the fingers pointing toward the feet and the thumbs under the neck.

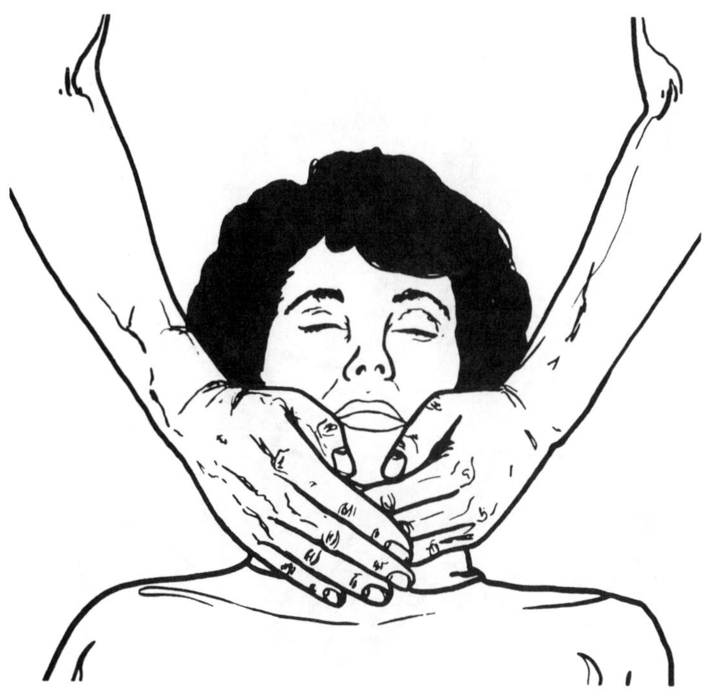

Position #4B

This is an alternate position. Add it if there is a problem in this area, or if your intuition guides you to use it. The hands are under the chin and over the throat. One hand is over the other. Use very light pressure.

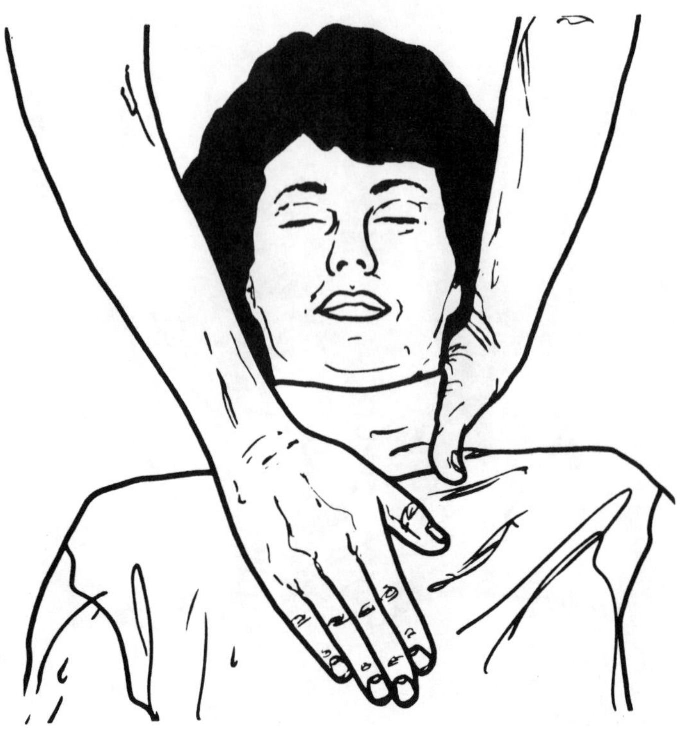

Position #5

Place your left hand under the neck and your right hand over the heart.

Hand Alignment for Stomach Positions

Place the fingers of one hand at the base of the other hand with either hand on top, whichever is most comfortable.

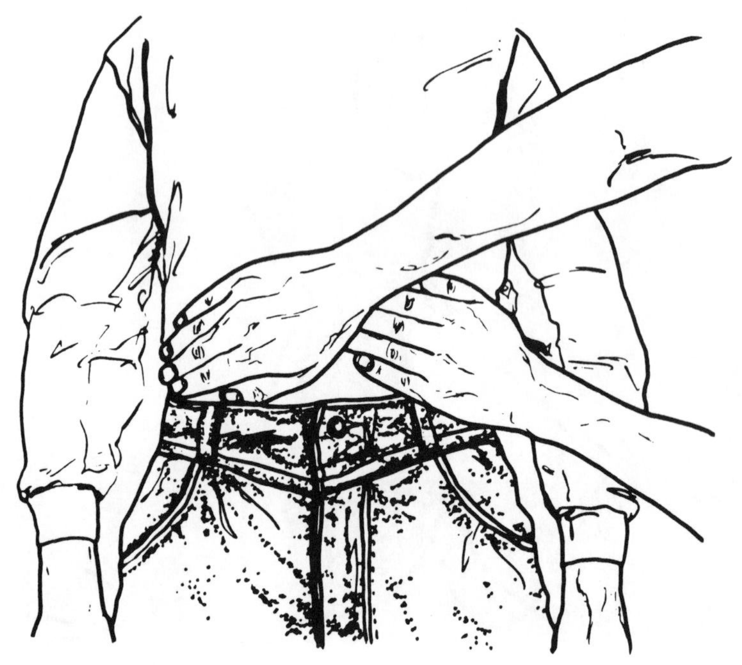

Position #6

Place your hands on the upper stomach along the ribs.

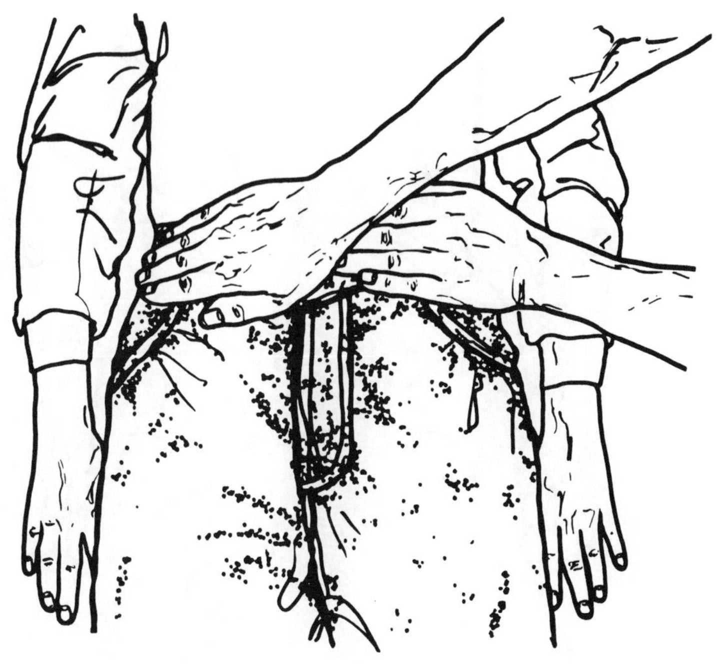

Position #7

Place your hands on the middle of the stomach across the navel area.

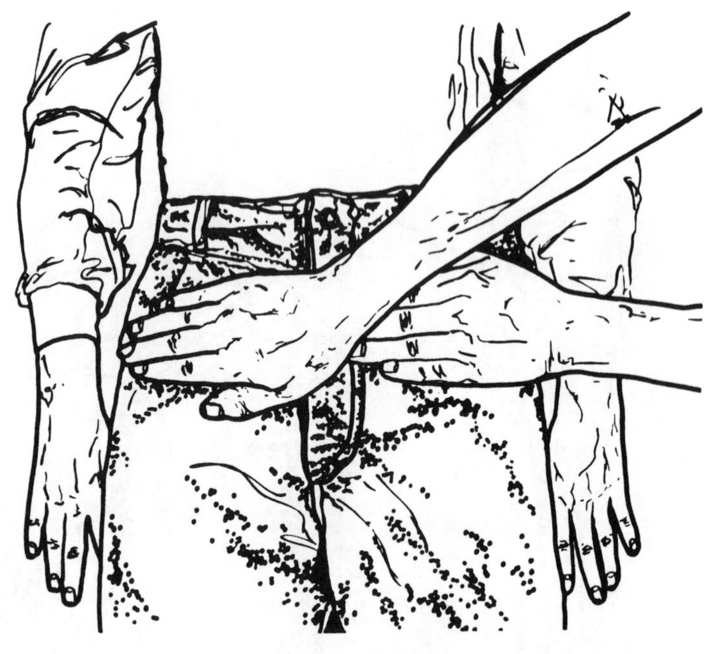

Position #8

Place your hands on the lower stomach across the hip bones.

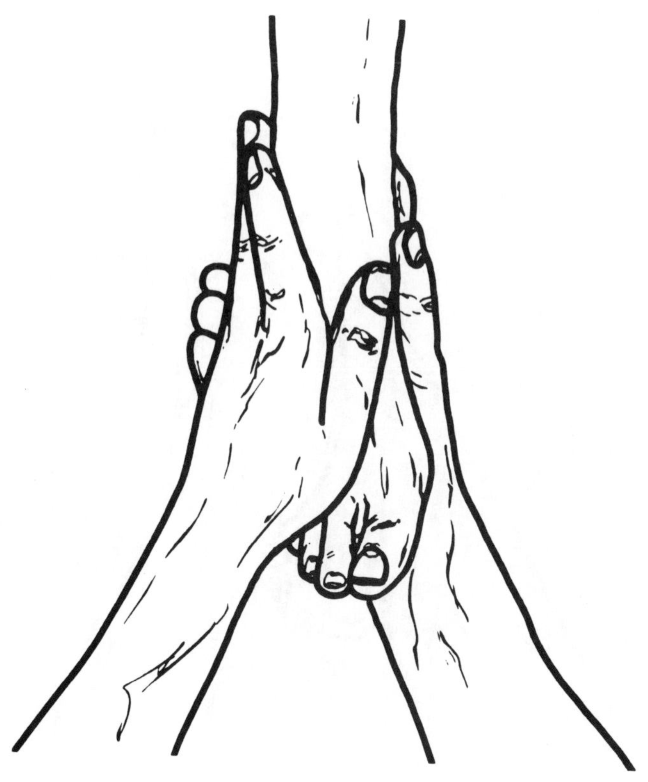

Position #9

Hold the right foot with both of your hands in a way that is comfortable for you.

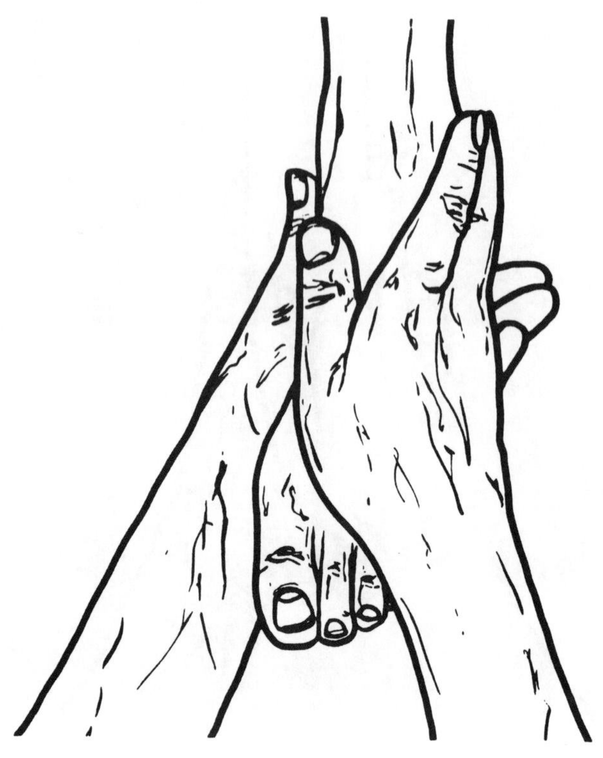

Position #10

Hold the left foot with both hands in a way that is comfortable for you.

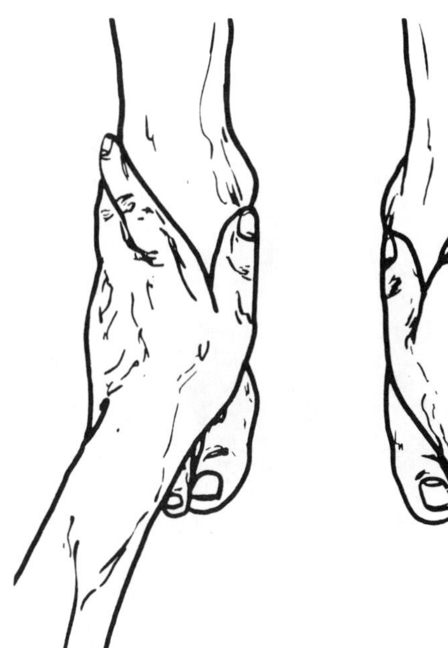

Position #11

Hold both feet in a way that is comfortable for you. You may feel guided to place your palms on the bottom of the feet.

If you used three to ten minutes for each position so far, the session will have lasted between forty-five minutes and an hour-and-a-half. You may go to Beaming now, or go on to treat the back. Continue with the back if the client has back problems, or if your intuition indicates to treat the back. Remember: Reiki directs itself and will often flow to places beyond where your hands are positioned. The back often receives Reiki when treating other parts of the body, especially when treating the feet.

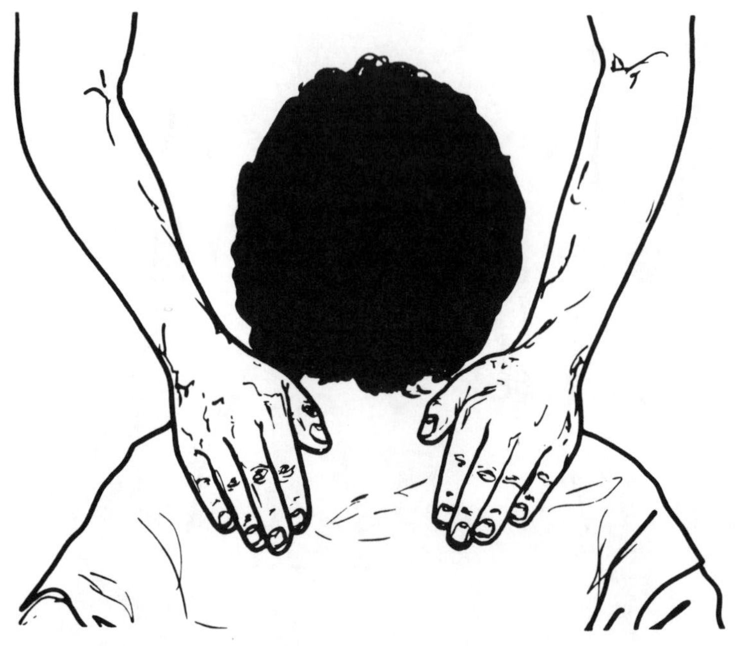

Position #12

Place your hands over the upper back.

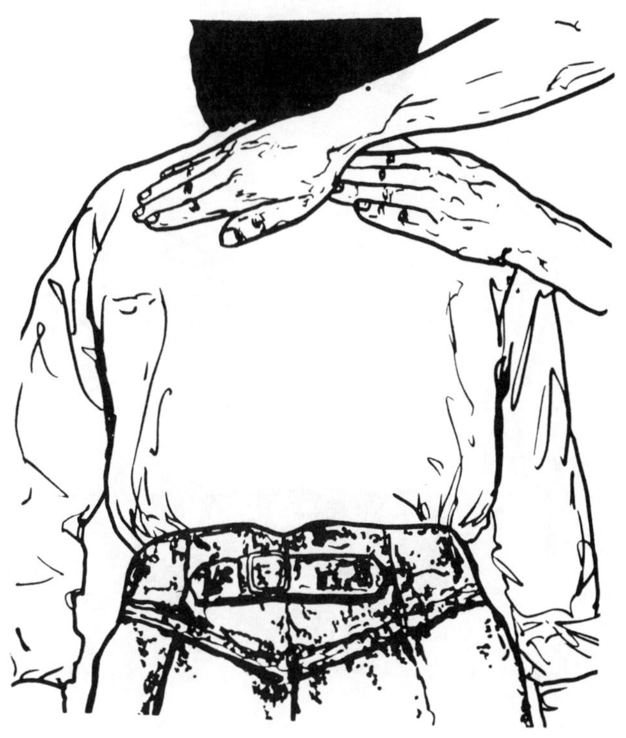

Position #13

Using the same hand alignment for the stomach as illustrated on page II-47, place your hands on the upper back.

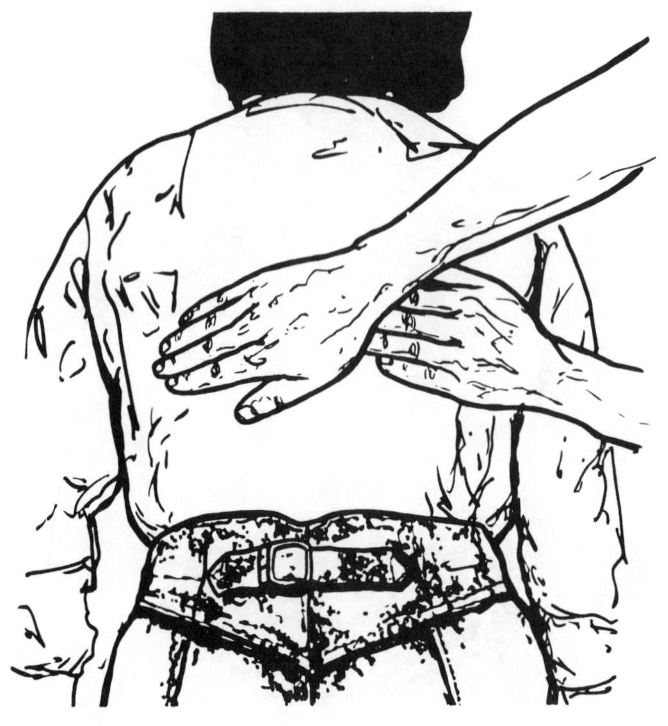

Position #14

Place your hands on the middle back.

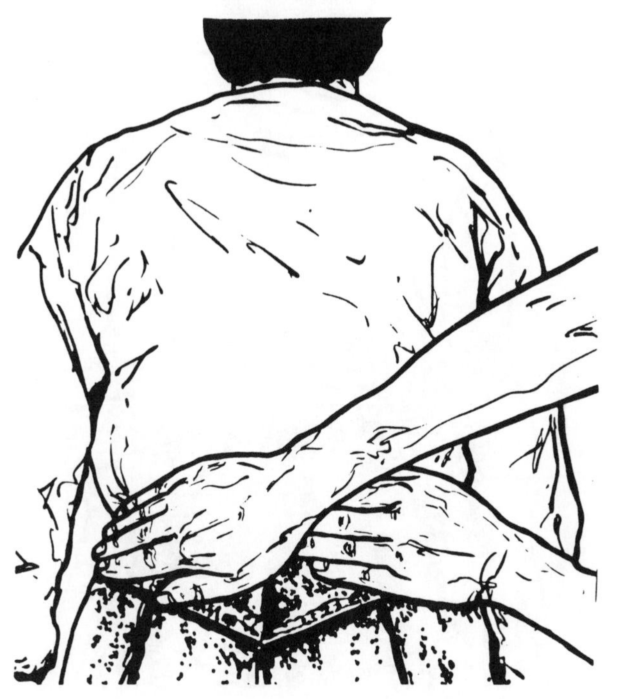

Position #15A

Place your hands on the lower back.

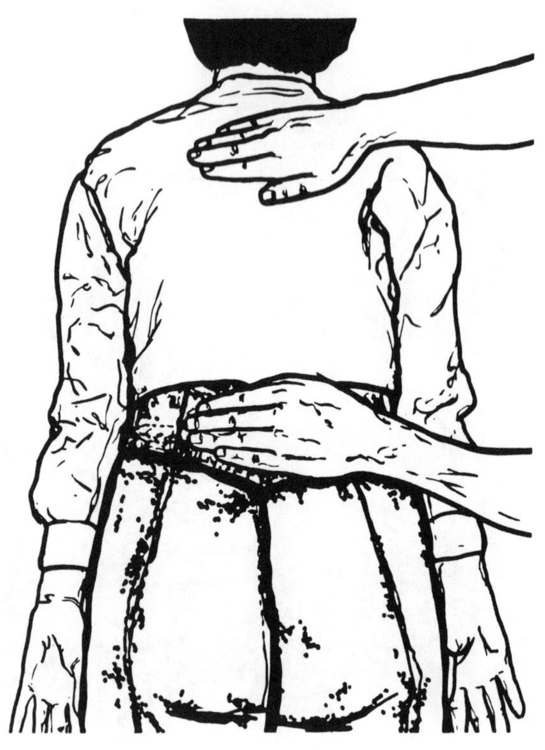

Position #15B

This is an alternate position and can be used if you feel guided to use it. Place your right hand behind the heart and your left hand on the base of the spine. You may also be directed to place your right hand on the crown of the head.

Chapter 9
Scanning and Beaming

Scanning and Beaming are two techniques I developed at the Center in 1990. They are based on dynamics exhibited by Reiki that were not being fully utilized at the time. They extend the effectiveness of a Reiki treatment, increasing awareness of where to treat and focusing healing in the aura where the cause of illness is found.

Scanning

The attunement process not only opens the palm chakras so that Reiki can flow, it also heightens their sensitivity to psychic energy. By using the chakras in the palms of your hands, it is possible to sense where a client needs Reiki. We call the process of finding and healing these areas of need "scanning".

To scan your client, first say a prayer asking to be guided to the places where the person needs Reiki. Then place your left (or non-dominant) hand about twelve inches away from the top of the person's head. Place your consciousness in the palm of your hand and notice how it feels. Then move your hand closer, about three to four inches from the top of the head, and begin moving your hand above the person's face and down toward the feet, continuing to remain about three to four inches away from the body. Move your hand very slowly and be aware of any changes in energy that register on the palm of your hand. When you feel any change at all, then you will know that this is a place where the person needs Reiki. You may feel coolness, warmth, tingling, pressure, little electric shocks, pulsations, distortions, irregularity or a pulling sensation. The change may be very slight and you may think it is in your imagination. However, trust your experience.

When you first begin to practice scanning, your sensitivity may not be very developed, so you need to pay very close attention. As you practice, your ability to scan the body will improve. After a while, you may even find that you can scan with your eyes and sense where the problems are, or you could begin to actually see the negative energy around the distressed areas.

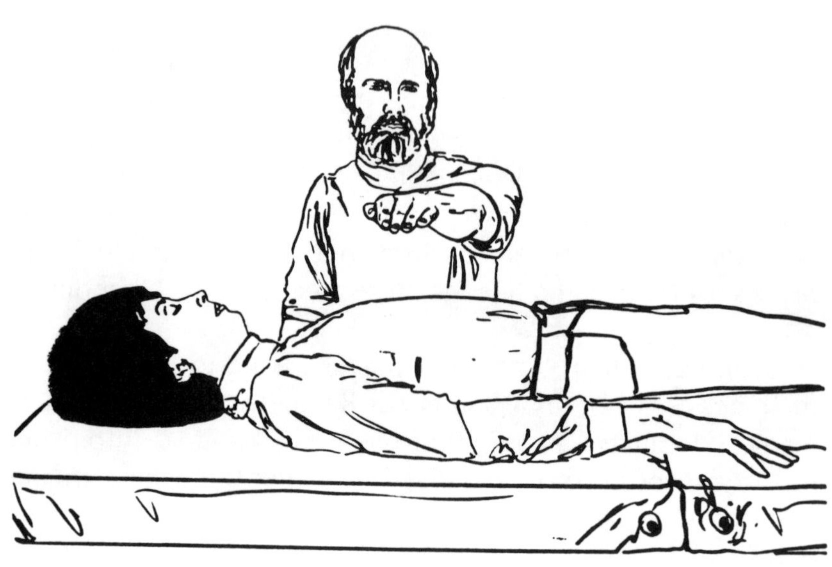

As soon as you find a change in the energy field, move your hand up and down until you find the height at which you feel the most distress. This could be as high as several feet above the body, or you may feel drawn to actually touch the body with your hands. Often the best height is found to be about four inches or so from the body.

When you find the right height, bring both hands together at this spot and channel Reiki. Reiki will heal the aura and chakra(s) and flow into the physical body to work on the organs and tissues and heal them also.

Continue channeling Reiki at the detected spot until you feel the flow of Reiki subsiding or until you feel the area is healed. Then re-scan the area to confirm that it is healed - if not, you can continue to do Reiki there until it feels complete. Afterwards, scan until you find another area in need of healing and do Reiki there. Continue until you have scanned and healed the whole energy field.

Scanning and healing the energy field is very healthy because the cause of most illnesses and other problems is in the aura. By treating the aura, you will be working on the cause and thereby healing problems before they can manifest in the physical body. Even after a problem has developed in the body, a client will respond better to Reiki if the aura is treated first. By healing the aura first, you will help the person's energy field to accept Reiki more completely. The energy will then flow more easily during the regular Reiki treatment. Therefore, if you are going to do both a scanning and a regular treatment, do the scanning first.

As you interact with the client's energy field, the two of you will become intimately connected. You may become aware of the cause of any distortion and the personal problems connected to it. You may also be given insight into how the problems were created and what the client can do to facilitate the healing. Share this information only if your are guided to do so, and then only with loving kindness and without judgment. This is sacred work. Always treat the client and the process with great respect.

Self-Scanning

The scanning process can also be done on yourself. Follow the same steps as above, looking for distortions and administering Reiki when you find them. Self-scanning can bring into consciousness aspects of yourself that you were not aware of. You will get to know yourself better and be shown new levels of yourself that need healing.

When you find a distortion in your energy field, ask what happened to create it and what you can do to help it heal. Remember, be kind to yourself. Accept whatever is shown to you without judgment or blame. Allow yourself to feel your feelings. Be ready to forgive and to let love in. This can be an intimate process, making you aware of deeper needs, increasing your sensitivity and facilitating personal growth.

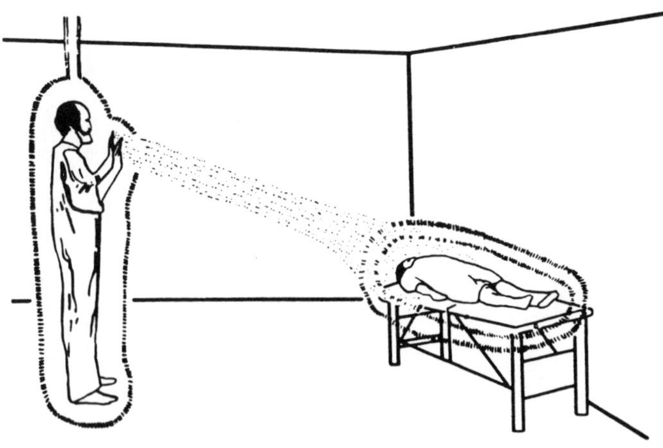

Beaming

At the Center we have developed a powerful method of channeling Reiki energy called Beaming. Using the distant healing symbol it is possible to beam Reiki to your client from across the room. This can dramatically increase the amount of Reiki flowing through you to the client. Beaming also creates a unique healing process of treating the whole aura at once. After treating the aura, the Reiki energy will enter the physical body and treat areas that need it.

It is also possible to beam Reiki directly to a specific area. Just imagine your hands are like radar dishes focusing Reiki on the area you want to treat. You can also direct it with your eyes.

Beaming works better if you allow your consciousness to merge with the Reiki consciousness. Simply be aware of the Reiki energy as it flows through you. Focus your mind only on the Reiki. If other thoughts come into your mind, gently brush them away and bring your attention back to the Reiki. By doing this, you will enter an altered state that allows the energy pathways Reiki flows through to open more than normal. It also allows your Reiki guides to more easily add their Reiki to yours. Beaming can be done at the end of a standard treatment or it can be done by itself.

Chapter 10
Giving a Complete Reiki Treatment

Before a client arrives you may want to clear and lighten up the energy in the room by burning some sage or using an essential oil. Candles are also helpful and create a nice ambiance.

1. Spend a few minutes talking with your client to gain rapport. Explain the Reiki process and the hand positions, and answer any questions the client may have. Ask the client to read and fill out the Client Information Form at the end of Appendix C.

2. Engage the client in goal-setting. There are several good ways to do this, as described at the end of the chapter.

3. To improve the effectiveness of the Reiki treatment, consider using the "Chanting Reiki Masters" tape available through our *Reiki News* (See Appendix D).

4. Wash your hands before and after the treatment. Make sure the client and you are both comfortable during the treatment. If you must sit in an uncomfortable position, it will slow the flow of Reiki. Especially make sure your arms and hands are relaxed. A Reiki table with chair will make giving a treatment more comfortable.

5. Before starting the treatment, ask the client to close his or her eyes and meditate on being thankful for, and open to, all the healing energies that are coming. You can also ask the client to focus on and accept any pleasant feelings that develop and to let go of all distress.

6. Sit quietly with your hands on your legs doing Reiki on yourself for a few moments. Then draw the power symbol down from the top of your head with the spiral near your root chakra so as to clear, protect, and empower you. You can also draw a smaller power symbol on each chakra starting with the root chakra and going up.

7. Make the power symbol in the middle of the room, and visualize it on the four walls, ceiling, and floor to clear the room of negative energies and fill the room with light. Then say a prayer asking your guides and the client's guides as well as the angels and all the healing forces of the Universe to work with you to protect the process and create the most powerful healing possible.

8. Draw the power symbol on each of your palms, and draw all three symbols over the client's heart, or draw the symbols over the client's crown chakra imagining them going through the crown and into the heart. As you do this, intend that all the energy from each symbol go wherever it is needed during the session.

9. Scan and treat the areas in the aura that need it. This will create unity in the person's energy field allowing Reiki to flow more strongly during the treatment.

10. Begin the standard treatment. Remember to draw or visualize the power symbol over any areas that need special attention. Also, visualize the power symbol *inside* the body within the organs or areas that need healing.

11. Stand back and beam Reiki toward the client. This is best done by moving five or six feet away so you are outside the client's aura.

12. While giving Reiki, meditate on being one with the Reiki energies. Your mind will be linked with the client's mind when giving a treatment so project positive thoughts to the client such as "I know I am healed, I know I am solving my problems," or any other affirmations you and the client have formulated.

13. End the treatment by sealing the client's energy field. To do this, draw the power symbol on the client's solar plexus, covering it briefly with your hand and saying to yourself, "I completely seal this Reiki treatment with divine love and wisdom." Brushing down the aura from the head to the feet also helps to complete the treatment.

14. After the client has gone, sit quietly doing Reiki on yourself. Visualize the power symbol on the walls and in the center of the room to clear and protect the room. Your Reiki energies will be high at this time so use them for your special projects, distant healing, etc.

Goal Setting to Enhance the Treatment

Here are a few additional things you can do to empower Reiki treatments, adding interest and making them more fun. You can do all of them or just a few. They can also be used in a self-treatment.

- Have clients write out the things that are not working in their lives. Include all areas of life. (This will cause the problems to come to the surface where Reiki can work more easily on them.) On another piece of paper, have them write out the goals and positive results they would like to achieve. Give them a few minutes by themselves to do this.

- Help them formulate affirmations to heal their problems and achieve their goals. Write the affirmations on another piece of paper. Take all three papers and put them into an envelope, and have your clients hold them while receiving the treatment. Be sure to use the mental/emotional symbol during the treatment to open the subconscious, and draw the symbol with your finger on each of the papers.

- During the treatment, have clients repeat the affirmations to themselves. While giving the treatment, imagine you are projecting the affirmations into them. Remember, during a Reiki treatment clients will be very open to positive suggestion, so this is a very powerful process.

- Make a symbolic ceremony of burning the papers in a metal bowl after the treatment. If doing this indoors, find a safe place and in any case keep a safe distance. Imagine the flames are transmuting the unwanted conditions into healing and that the goals are being empowered. During the burning, hold your hands toward the flames and have clients do the same. Secretly visualize Reiki symbols in the flames and if clients have had Reiki II, encourage them to join you in the visualization. Have the clients take the ashes home and bury them in their garden. The idea is that the negative things are being buried and composted so the positive things the clients are planting can grow.

Part III

Your Own Reiki Practice

The Promise of a Developing Reiki Practice

People come to you with many different problems, difficulties and illnesses, sometimes as a last resort, and you watch them leave relaxed, often radiant with joy and new hope . . . seeing them improve over time, watching them grow, gain confidence and become more trusting of life . . . seeing some make major changes and life adjustments . . . occasionally witnessing miracles . . . feeling the wonder of God's love pass through you and into another . . . sensing the presence of spiritual beings, feeling their touch, and knowing they work with you . . . being raised into ever greater levels of joy and peace by simply placing your hands on another . . . watching your life grow and develop as your continual immersion in Reiki transforms your attitudes, values and beliefs . . . sensing that because of your commitment to help others, beings of light are focusing their love and healing on you and carefully guiding you on your spiritual path. All this is the promise of a developing Reiki practice!

Chapter 11
Developing Your Reiki Practice

Reiki is a truly wonderful gift, and after taking your first Reiki class it is important to do Reiki on yourself, then on friends and family. After doing this awhile and gaining experience and confidence, you may feel inspired to share it with a much wider circle of people.

The development of a Reiki practice can be very rewarding. Not only can it provide you with a source of income; there are spiritual experiences that can be much more meaningful. So, assuming you have been initiated into Reiki and have taken time to gain experience in its use, I would like to share some ideas and techniques that may be helpful in developing a Reiki practice.

Intention Is the Most Important Thing

The most important thing concerning the development of a Reiki practice is the quality and strength of your intention. The mind is like a magnet. The quality and strength of your thoughts will determine the quality and strength of what you attract into your life. Therefore it is important for you to develop and maintain a positive mental attitude about your Reiki practice.

Decide with clarity, determination and commitment that you are going to create a thriving Reiki practice. Decide that you are worthy to do this and that there are many people who will benefit from your service. Decide that the value you and your clients receive from your Reiki practice will far outweigh any effort or sacrifice that might be involved in creating it.

Picture in your mind the results you want to create and how it will feel when you are actively involved in a thriving Reiki practice. Meditate frequently on this image and these feelings. Allow them to fill you up and surround you and reach out to others. Use this to motivate you and to help you keep on in the face of doubt or discouragement. Know in your heart that having your own Reiki practice is a valid goal that will bring freedom, joy and satisfaction, and that you are creating it now! Believe in yourself and in your purpose!

If doubts arise about your goal, know that this is normal and assume that they have entered your mind only because they are passing out of you. Whenever we take on a new level of healing or commit to a new goal, old negative thoughts and feelings that have been stored inside and have gone unchallenged are dislodged and begin to move through our consciousness. If your commitment is strong, these old negative feelings and thoughts will break up and be released. Experiencing negative feelings and thoughts is often part of the healing process, so just release them up to the Higher Power to be healed. Use Reiki to speed up this process and make sure to ask for treatments from others. Reiki aura clearing can be especially helpful at this point.

Compassion Brings Help from Higher Sources

There are higher sources of help you can call on as well. Angels, beings of light and Reiki spirit guides as well as your own enlightened self are available to help you. They can help you develop your Reiki practice by directing clients to you and assisting with treatments. They can be of great benefit, but you must have a strong spiritual intention for your work if you are to recruit their aid. If you are doing Reiki in a selfish way, only for money or to gain control over others or to take on an air of self-importance, or for any other negative purpose, then it will be very difficult for these spiritual beings to work with you. There must be congruence, a spiritual alignment within you, in order for the Higher Power in the form of Reiki to flow through you in a powerful way and in order for the angels, Reiki spirit guides and other spiritual beings to work with you. Reiki wants only the best for you, but you must align yourself with the nature of Reiki if you are to gain the greatest benefit. The more you can open to the true nature of Reiki, which is to have an unselfish heart centered desire to help others, the more the Reiki spirit guides can help you. Focus on helping others and on healing anything within yourself that may inhibit the flow of love and compassion. This is what will make your Reiki practice a success!

The development of a spiritual attitude toward your Reiki practice can be facilitated through the regular use of affirmations and prayers. Try the following prayer: "Guide me and heal me so that I can be of greater service to others." By sincerely saying a prayer such as this each day, your heart will open and a path will be created to receive the help of higher spiritual beings. They will guide you in your Reiki practice and in the development of your life purpose.

Competitiveness Is Not a Part of Reiki

One thing that can get in the way of developing a spiritual attitude about your Reiki practice is fear of competition. This has caused more problems and created more restrictions and negative energy in the Reiki community than any other area of misunderstanding. Lack is an illusion and this is especially true for Reiki! There are far more people who need healing on the planet than there are Reiki practitioners to assist them. Fear of competition goes directly against the nature of Reiki energy and because of this, it can repel people from you who might otherwise be interested in receiving a treatment. Competitiveness depends on the illusion of separate existence, but Reiki expresses the power of wholeness, which is divine love in action. People who do Reiki together find that their Reiki gets stronger as more people join the group. If Reiki were competitive, then just the opposite would happen: it would be strongest when you were alone and grow weaker as more people joined the group.

The nature of Reiki energy is one of cooperation. It understands the reality that we are all one and it flows freely to anyone and everyone. It works in harmony with all other forms of treatment. Therefore, it is Reiki wisdom to welcome all other practitioners as allies. If the spiritual purpose for your Reiki practice is to help others and to heal the planet, then you can only rejoice when you hear about other Reiki practitioners in your area because they are helping you fulfill that purpose. Accept the wisdom of Reiki as your own wisdom; believe that all others who practice Reiki are helping you. The more you can do this, the more your Reiki practice will thrive.

Don't worry about taking clients away from other practitioners. Each practitioner has value and a special way of helping others. You will attract the clients who are right for you. Others will attract the clients who are right for them.

Reiki Will Soon Be in Great Demand

An important trend is developing in society that will soon create a great demand for Reiki practitioners. More and more people are discovering the value of complementary therapy. A recent study conducted by David M. Eisenberg, M.D. of Boston's Beth Israel Hospital indicates that people in the U.S. are beginning to turn away from modern medicine and make greater use of complementary health care. The survey found that one-third of all Americans used at least one form of complementary therapy in 1990 and that they spent nearly

$14 billion for this treatment, most of it out of pocket. The therapies most often used were meditation, touch therapy (such as Reiki), guided imagery, spiritual healing, chiropractic, hypnosis, homeopathy, acupuncture, herbal cures, and folk remedies.[1] Also of note is the fact that the National Institutes of Health have created an Office of Alternative Medicine (OAM, toll free number 888-644-6226) whose purpose is to research complementary healing methods and establish their value. Many healing techniques formerly considered quackery by the American medical establishment have been proven valid by this new office. So far the OAM has validated the worth of chiropractic, acupuncture and homeopathy, and will begin studying touch therapy and Reiki soon.

Clearly, a paradigm shift is taking place toward the general acceptance of complementary medical treatment. It is likely Reiki will become widely accepted as a valid form of healing before the end of the decade! It is already being used in hospitals and doctors' offices. (See Appendix B.) Think what this means for anyone with a Reiki practice. A great need is developing for Reiki practitioners!

The Practical Issue of Money

Now that we have covered some of the important attitudes, values and beliefs necessary for a thriving Reiki practice, let's discuss some of the practical issues. An important issue is money. Some practitioners do not charge money and this is fine. You have the right to charge whatever you want, or to charge nothing at all. However, it is often better for clients if they are able to give something in return. When people receive a treatment for free they often feel indebted to the practitioner and feelings of guilt can develop. This creates an imbalance that can get in the way of continued treatments. Charging money allows people the freedom to come whenever they want. If you have clients with money problems, you can charge them less or work out some bartering arrangement. It is also fine to do free treatments for those who cannot pay. Those who do pay are not paying for the Reiki energy which is free, but for the time and effort you have put forth to learn Reiki.

How much should you charge for a Reiki session? A good rule of thumb is to charge about the same for a Reiki session as others in your area are charging for massage. A Reiki session will usually last about forty-five minutes to an hour-and-a-half. When you first start charging for sessions you can start at a lower rate if that feels more comfortable to you, and then increase it as your confidence and reputation grow.

Advertise Your Practice

Business cards are a good first step when starting your practice. They let people know you are serious about your Reiki business and make it easy for you to give people your phone number in case they want to make an appointment. It is *not* a good idea to place your address on the card as people may come without calling you. It is a good idea to talk to people first to get a feel for their energy, and to let them know what they can expect from a Reiki session, before setting an appointment and giving them directions to your home or office.

Flyers are also a good idea. In your flyer explain what Reiki is and does; also give your name and phone number. You can place the flyers on bulletin boards in health food stores, new age book stores, etc., and can give them to prospective clients.

Beginning your Reiki practice in your home is a good idea as it will save money on start-up costs, but many practitioners have found advantages to having their own office. An office creates a professional atmosphere and lets people know that you take your work seriously. You may want to start in your home and move into an office after things get going, or if you can afford it, get an office right away. Consider the fact that you may want to have group activities in your office when considering the size office you want. Perhaps you can share your space with another complementary therapist to reduce your overhead.

Keep a Mailing List

Make sure to get each client's name, address and phone number for your mailing list. As your list continues to grow, you can mail out flyers on upcoming Reiki events or simply send out little reminders about your practice. A good way to keep track of your clients is to use a client information form. The one in Appendix C of this book is good because it includes a disclaimer which protects you from any misunderstandings that could develop about the results a person can expect from a Reiki session. Feel free to make copies of this form and use it in your practice. Stay on the lookout for other ways of adding people with an interest in complementary healing to your mailing list. The mailing list can be an important tool in promoting your Reiki practice.

Exchange Treatments

One way to let people know about your Reiki practice is to offer to exchange Reiki with other complementary therapists. This works well with massage therapists as they are familiar with body work and often need therapy themselves. Offer to refer clients to them and ask them to do the same for you. Give them some of your flyers or business cards to display in their office.

Give Impromptu Demonstrations

When you are at public gatherings or around others and people complain about an ache or pain, offer to give them Reiki. If they have never heard of Reiki before, explain that it is a Japanese form of stress reduction with many healing benefits. If they have a metaphysical understanding you can talk about Ki and life energy. Talk to them on a level they can understand. Take fifteen minutes or so to treat the area of concern, let them know you do this professionally and give them your business card. Tell them what a complete session is like and set up an appointment if they are interested. At parties or large gatherings, the attention you attract when giving Reiki to one person often creates interest in others who will want a sample treatment also. Often you end up treating several people and passing out many business cards. As you treat you can talk about Reiki and how it works. Ask those you treat to explain what they feel. This always creates a lot of interest. Being focused on helping people and not on getting clients is the key to attracting people for sample treatments. However, if they are interested, giving them a business card is appropriate.

One thing that will really attract attention for your Reiki practice is wearing a Reiki T-shirt. People will want to know what the symbols mean and this opens the door to talking about Reiki. Offer to give them a sample treatment and tell them about your practice. If they seem interested, give them a business card and if possible, set up an appointment.

Offer Free Reiki Evenings

A free Reiki evening can create lots of interest. Plan one night a month to talk about Reiki and give sample treatments. If you have Reiki friends, ask them to come and help give treatments. This is a great way to help others and to let them know about

Reiki and your practice. Make up flyers for your free Reiki evening and put them up in appropriate places. If the Reiki practitioners can meet an hour or so before the meeting to give treatments to each other it will really improve the quality of what the non-Reiki people receive. Also, if you have taken Reiki III/Master training, you could give a refresher attunement or healing attunement to each of the practitioners to boost their energy. This is a great way for all to practice their Reiki and for you to practice giving attunements. Call and invite everyone you know who would be interested.

If your area has psychic or holistic fairs, get a booth. Take a Reiki table and ask five or more of your Reiki friends to help. Offer ten or fifteen minute treatments with five or more Reiki practitioners giving a treatment to one person at a time. Charge $10.00 or so per treatment. This can be a powerful healing experience and a good demonstration of Reiki. Have a table with your flyers and business cards on it and be sure to get each person's name, address, and phone number for your mailing list. Another way is to use chairs and to have one or two practitioners give ten or fifteen minute treatments to each person. The chair method takes up less space and allows you to treat more than one person at a time.

Offer Reiki as a Public Service

Create a healing service at your church. Recruit other healers to help. You could use both Reiki and non-Reiki healers. This can create tremendous interest in Reiki. Refer to the Summer 93 issue of the *Reiki News,* see the *Reiki News* Article booklet or consult our web site at www.reiki.org for a complete description of this program.

Volunteer to do free Reiki treatments at hospitals (see Appendix B, which contains the article "Reiki In Hospitals" from the Winter 97 issue of the *Reiki News*). You may also want to donate treatments at hospice centers, drug and alcohol treatment centers or in conjunction with a psychologist or other therapists. By doing this, you will gain experience and people will find out about your practice, but most of all, you will be helping others.

Deliver Talks on Reiki

Develop a Reiki talk and offer to speak about Reiki to local groups. There are many groups looking for speakers, and complementary healing is becoming a hot topic. If you have little experience at public speaking, you can join a local Toastmasters Club. There you will be coached and given ample opportunity to develop your speaking ability. If you are making Reiki your career, then the ability to speak before groups is a must. Decide to become a great speaker and go for it.

Cultivate the Media

If there is a metaphysical/holistic paper in your area, offer to write an article on Reiki or on healing in general. Make sure your name and phone number are listed and indicate that you are a Reiki practitioner or teacher. If you are really serious, decide to write an article every issue. This will let people know who you are and what your attitudes and beliefs are concerning healing. They will then be able to decide if they want to come to you. It is a good idea to place an ad in the same paper that carries your article. You will pay for the ad, but the article will be free!

Write articles for the *Reiki News* or send in a description of your Reiki experiences. The *Reiki News* needs articles and is very interested in letting people know about your personal experiences with Reiki. It goes out to more than 72,000 people who are interested in Reiki all over the world. Having your name in the paper will improve your reputation, especially if you place free copies in your local health and new age book stores and hand out copies to your clients and friends, etc.

In many parts of the country the news media are reporting the positive benefits of alternative healing. So, call the local newspapers and TV stations. Find out which reporter(s) are in charge of or interested in information about complementary healing. Talk to them and let them know you are a Reiki practitioner/teacher. Explain Reiki to them in a way they can understand - tell them it is a Japanese form of stress reduction and relaxation that also promotes healing. Tell them there are over 1,000,000 practitioners in the U.S. and the numbers are growing! Give them details and make it interesting and exciting. Offer to give them a free treatment. Let them know that you are available should they decide to write an article or air a program about Reiki or alternative healing, or if any questions come up about it in the future. Establish in their mind that you are an expert on Reiki. They will then think of you as a resource person. Most reporters keep a file of people they can call on for different subjects and they will probably put your name in it! If they are not ready to do a story now, when they are ready it is likely they will call you!

Become Licensed through the Center

Become a licensed Reiki Master/Teacher through the International Center for Reiki Training. When you do this, we will list your classes in the newsletter and refer students and clients to you. Your classes will also be eligible to give Continuing Education Units (CEUs) to nurses, massage therapists and body workers. The Center continually receives requests from people all over the country who are interested in Reiki sessions and classes. If you are licensed by the Center, we can refer these prospective clients to you. (See Appendix C to obtain a booklet about Center licensing requirements.)

Assume Success

If you are beginning to teach and are having trouble getting a class together, simply plan a class, set a date and assume the class will be full. Then when you tell people about the class, they will pick up a positive attitude from you about the class and will want to come. If people sense a tentativeness, it will discourage them from attending. Being decisive about your plans and having a positive attitude will attract students and bring the class together. Your guides will also be better able to work with you if you are clear about what you intend to do. Remember to visualize yourself being successful. Be enthusiastic about your plans and send Reiki to your goals everyday!

These ideas have worked for others, and they will work for you. Try them! Also, use your intuition to develop other ways to promote your Reiki practice. Remember, a clear intention is the first step to success. Keep track of the results you get with each activity you try. Keep using the ones that work and drop the ones that don't. Keep trying new ideas until you get the results you want. By following this formula you will create a successful Reiki practice and in so doing, bring joy, peace and healing to others.

[1] Eisenberg, David, et al. "Unconventional Medicine in the United States." *New England Journal of Medicine* 328, no. 4 (1993), 246-52.

Whatsoever thou resolvest to do, do it quickly. Defer not till the evening what the morning may accomplish.
Unto Thee I Grant

Chapter 12
Becoming a Reiki Master

Reiki is a sacred practice that requires reverence and our greatest respect if we are to experience its full value. The benefits of Reiki can be all-encompassing, not only giving us the ability to heal ourselves and others, which by itself is deeply meaningful, but also bringing guidance for our lives. Its unlimited nature can create opportunities for continual growth and unfoldment of our boundless potential. The ever increasing joy, peace and abundance that await those who sincerely pursue the path of Reiki are not only a blessing to be enjoyed, but also contain the healing the planet so dearly needs. Those who have been initiated into Reiki often feel this greater potential and aspire to continue to the Advanced and Master levels.

The desire to grow is inherent in simply being alive. As we look around ourselves and observe other living things, we can clearly see that all living things share the impulse to grow. Because this is what living things do, one could even say that the purpose of life is to grow and develop. Therefore, the desire to grow in one's Reiki potential is a natural expression of one's core essence and of life itself. If you feel this desire in your heart, honor and respect it. Doing so will fulfill an innate need.

Reiki - A Joyful Path

The joys of becoming a Reiki Master are many and you don't necessarily have to teach in order for the Master training offered by the Center to be useful. The additional healing energy, symbols, techniques and knowledge will add value to your healing abilities. Treating yourself and treating others in person and at a distance will all be noticeably improved. The fact that you can pass Reiki on to friends and family is also a definite plus. Many take the Master training with just this in mind. However, if you ever decide to formally teach, you will be able to do so. As you take the Center's Reiki Master training and increase your personal vibration, this adds to the vibration of the whole planet!

One of the greatest joys of Reiki Mastership is teaching Reiki to others. Imagine the thrill of witnessing the members of your Reiki class receiving Reiki energy during the attunement and then, as you guide them in its use, sharing in their joy and amazement as they experience its gentle power flowing through them for the first time. As your students use Reiki to help family, friends and clients, a wonderful sense of spiritual connection will develop among all of you. Feelings of compassion and love for everyone will be strengthened as you merge with the Reiki consciousness and know more deeply than ever before that we all come from God and that we are all one in God.

What Is a Reiki Master?

The definition of a teaching Reiki Master according to the Center is anyone who has received the Master attunement and master symbol and who understands how to give all the attunements. In order to be considered a Reiki Master, one must also have taught Reiki to at least one other person. Those who have taken Reiki Master training but not taught Reiki to anyone would not qualify as Reiki Masters so far as the Center is concerned and should call themselves Reiki Master practitioners instead until they do begin to teach.

Master Training Is a Serious Step

Becoming a Reiki Master is a serious step that requires definite preparation. One must first take Reiki I & II and Advanced Reiki Training. Practice using Reiki is absolutely necessary. Experience with the energy and using the symbols is a must. It is also necessary to meditate on your life purpose and decide if Reiki Mastership is in harmony with it. Then, it is important to study with a competent and compatible Reiki Master who will encourage and help you after you become a Reiki Master.

How to Find the Right Teacher

Before taking Reiki Master training, you should ask your prospective teacher exactly what you will be able to *do* after you are trained. Will you receive the complete training and be able to initiate others into all the degrees including full Reiki Master? Or will something be left out, requiring you to take additional sub-levels or degrees and pay additional fees? Because of changes some have made to the system of Reiki, this is a very important question to ask. If you choose to study with one of the Center's Licensed Teachers, you will receive the complete Reiki Master training.

Becoming a Reiki Master implies the ability to initiate others into Reiki. Therefore, it is important to find a teacher who will spend time in class helping you practice the attunement processes used in the initiations. Ask potential teachers how much time is spent in class practicing the attunements, as some teachers spend little or none. Also ask them how much support they are willing to give you to begin teaching your own classes. This is important. Some Reiki Masters will have little interest in helping you get started, as they are afraid you will take students away from them. If you are serious about becoming a successful teaching Reiki Master, find a teacher who will openly support you in achieving your goal.

After taking the Master training, and before teaching your first class, additional practice doing the attunements is a good idea. This can be done on friends who already have Reiki. Ask them if they would like to be "attunement models" and let them know that the additional attunements will be beneficial for them and will refine and strengthen their Reiki energies. Most will gladly agree. If you can't find someone to practice on, you can use a teddy bear or a pillow to represent a person.

It will also be necessary to practice the talks, lectures and meditations you will be leading in class. Make outlines of your talks and practice reading them into a tape recorder. Listen to your tapes and take notes on ways you can improve your talks. Then continue to practice until you are confident. Don't be afraid to use your outline in class. When teaching, relax and let the Reiki energy do the work.

If you have a sincere desire to help others and have taken the time to prepare, you should have no trouble attracting students. It is your attitude that creates the results you receive, so assume success and you will create success.

Treat Students with Great Respect

As a teaching Reiki Master it is important to treat your students with the greatest respect. Know that all have the spark of God within them. Never use subtle threats or withhold information to make your students dependent on you. Openly encourage all students to be connected to their own power and freedom of choice. What you create for others comes back to you. As you truly empower others, so will you be empowered. Trust in the abundance of the Universe and you will receive abundance. You will also be blessed with peace and joy.

Set a Good Example

When teaching Reiki to others, it is important to set a good example by being an authentic representative of Reiki energy. People cannot be so easily fooled by surface spirituality now. They want and need a real teacher who comes from experience and is working on her or his own deep healing. This requires one to meditate on the nature of Reiki energy and surrender to it. It is a continual process of working with all aspects of one's being that are out of step with Reiki energy and allowing the energy to heal them. We must seek to develop and express the qualities of love, compassion, wisdom, justice, cooperation, humility, persistence, kindness, courage, strength and abundance, as Reiki energy is all of these and more. It may seem paradoxical, but it is true that a real Reiki Master is one who is always becoming a Reiki Master. Like life itself, it is a process of continual growth.

As you do this, you will realize sooner or later that there is more to Reiki than using it to heal yourself and others of specific problems. Reiki has a deeper purpose. In the same way that Reiki is able to guide healing energy when you are giving a treatment, Reiki can guide your life.

Your Life Purpose

There is a perfect plan for your life that has always been present and waiting for you. This plan is exactly what is good and right and healthy for *you*. This plan is not based on what your parents want for you, or what the culture says you need to do to be accepted. It is based on what will really make you happy.

This plan is inside of you and comes from your core essence. Reiki can activate and help you follow this plan, which is your true spiritual path.

By treating yourself and others and by meditating on the essence of Reiki, you will be guided more and more by Reiki in making important decisions. Sometimes you will find yourself doing things that don't seem to make sense or conform to what you think you should be doing, and sometimes you will be guided to do things that you have told yourself you would never do. However, by trusting more and more in the guidance of Reiki, by letting go of what your ego thinks it needs to be happy and by humbly surrendering to Reiki's loving power, you will find your life changing in ways that bring greater harmony and feelings of real happiness.

The Way of Reiki

Over time, you will learn from experience that the guidance of Reiki is worthy of your trust. Once you have surrendered completely, you will have entered The Way of Reiki. When you do this, you will be at peace with the past, have complete faith in the future and know that there never was anything to worry about. Your life will work with ever greater harmony, and you will feel that you have reached your goal of wholeness even as you continue to move toward it!

In the end, we must consider that a Reiki Master is not one who has mastered Reiki, but one whom Reiki has mastered. This requires that we surrender completely to the spirit of Reiki, allowing it to guide every area of our lives and become our only focus and source of nurturing and sustenance.

As we proceed into the next millennium, The Way of Reiki offers itself as a solution to our problems and as a path of unlimited potential. May all who would benefit from this path be guided to it.

Appendices

Appendix A

Discovering the Roots of Reiki

Discovering the Roots of Reiki

by William Lee Rand and Laura Ellen Gifford

As teachers and practitioners of Reiki we have enjoyed sharing the "traditional" story of the history of Reiki as it has been taught to us in the West. However, this story has never felt complete to us, and many others have told us they felt the same way. Important information seemed to be missing, and parts of the story didn't seem to fit. Some of the "facts," upon investigation, proved to be untrue, and much of the rest of the story could not be verified.

The information available in the West about Dr. Usui, or Usui Sensei as he is called by Reiki students in Japan, has been so limited and larger-than-life that some people have wondered if he ever really existed at all. This has made it difficult to feel connected to him and to the roots of the system he created.

Last year we published an article on the "Original Reiki Ideals" which revealed a more authentic version of the ideals we had been given in the West. Since then, additional information has been uncovered from the investigations of Dave King, Melissa Riggall, Robert Jefford and others. The most interesting and verifiable of this new information is from Frank Arjava Petter in his new book, *Reiki Fire*. Arjava was one of the first Western Reiki Masters to teach other Masters in Japan, which he has done since 1993.

Japanese Sources for Reiki History

With the help of his Japanese wife Chetna and Japanese Reiki Master Shizuko Akimoto, Arjava contacted a number of people who have proved to be important sources of information about the history of Reiki. Two of these, Tsutomo Oishi and

Fumio Ogawa,[1] learned Reiki from a Master who had been taught by Usui Sensei himself. Arjava also spoke to members of Usui Sensei's family and to members of the Usui Shiki Reiki Ryoho, the original Reiki organization started by Usui Sensei in Tokyo. From these contacts he filled in some missing information on the history of Reiki and discovered other valuable facts. This information provides more accurate insight into who Usui Sensei was, what motivated him to rediscover Reiki and how he and his students practiced.

After reading Arjava's book, we were interested in knowing more and e-mailed him with many questions. He answered our questions and invited us to Japan to visit the sacred sites and discuss the implications of this new information. We gladly accepted and flew to Japan the second week of September 1997.

Our Trip to Japan

Many synchronicities occurred in connection with our trip to Japan, starting with someone faxing us important pages from Arjava's book. Before and after our trip was scheduled, we met people who lived in Japan who offered to act as additional guides for us.

Just two weeks after we met on the Internet, Friedemann Greulich traveled from Japan to the University of Kentucky on business and visited Laura at her Healing Center in Kentucky to exchange Reiki sessions. At this time we had not planned our trip to Japan. It turned out that Friedemann lives only 10 minutes from where Arjava lives in Japan and he offered to help us at Mt. Kurama!

Another person, Yuki Yamamoto, flew from Osaka to the Center to attend a Karuna Reiki® class, knowing nothing about our planned trip. Osaka is close to Mt. Kurama and Yuki had been there many times. When he found out about our trip, he offered to join us at Mt. Kurama with his car and be our guide.

So, without seeking it, we had several extra guides that proved to be very helpful! We feel these things happened as a result of our daily Reiki practice during which we invite the energy to guide every aspect of our lives.

Mt. Kurama - Where Reiki was Rediscovered

According to literature at the Mt. Kurama Temple, in 770 A.D. a priest named Gantei climbed Mount Kurama, led by a white horse. His soul was enlightened with the realization of Bishamon-ten, the protector of the northern quarter of the Buddhist heaven and the spirit of the sun. Gantei founded the Buddhist Temple on Mt. Kurama which went through many stages of development and restoration and now contains many temples and pagodas. The temple was formerly part of the Tendai sect of Buddhism. Since 1949, it has been part of the newly founded Kurama-Kokyo sect of Buddhism.

Arjava, Yuki and Friedemann accompanied us to Mt. Kurama during our several trips to the mountain. Mt. Kurama has wonderful energy! The Kurama Temples are located up the side of the mountain, requiring that one hike up and down the mountain to visit them. This would normally be very tiring, but we found that taking a moment to rest there quickly restores one's energy. Mt. Kurama is truly a "power spot" and the energy that flows is very uplifting, yet calming. There is a feeling of contentment and peace. We both were aware of many helpful spirits from whom we received inspiration and guidance.

Our first stop up the mountain was at the San-mon Station. There is a shrine here representing the Trinity which, in the

Kurama-Kokyo Buddhist sect, is known as Sonten or Supreme Deity. Sonten is thought to be the source of all creation - the essence of all that is. Sonten is said to have come to Earth over six million years ago in the form of Mao-son, the great king of the conquerors of evil, who descended upon Mt. Kurama from Venus. His mission was the salvation and evolution of mankind and all living things on earth. Mao-son is also said to have incarnated as the Spirit of the Earth, residing inside an ancient cedar tree at the top of the mountain. This spirit is thought to emanate from Mount Kurama to this day. Sonten manifests on Earth as Love, Light and Power.

Roots of the Reiki Symbols

The love symbol is called Senju-Kannon and looks very similar to the Usui mental/emotional symbol. It is the Sanskrit seed syllable *hrih*. The light symbol is called Bishamon-ten and is represented by the Sanskrit seed syllable *vai*. The power symbol is called Mao-son and is represented by the Sanskrit seed syllable *hum*. The essence of all three is in each one. It is interesting to note the similarity between these three symbols and the symbols of Reiki II. Pictures of these symbols are on page I-36.

The kanji for the Usui master symbol is also used in the Kurama Temple literature. The meaning of Sonten is expressed using the same kanji we use for the Usui master symbol. During a temple prayer in the Hondon Temple, we were given special permission to be present as the priest used the name of the Usui master symbol during part of his chant!

It has to be more than a coincidence that the Usui master symbol is used by the Kurama Temple to represent Sonten, the Supreme Deity, and that the symbol which represents love looks very similar to the Usui mental/emotional symbol. Since

Usui Sensei received his Reiki initiation on Mt. Kurama, it is likely he made use of some of the symbolism and philosophy of the Kurama Temple in the formulation of Reiki.

In fact, the understanding we received from Shizuko Akimoto is that Usui Sensei studied many things before rediscovering Reiki. He took what he studied and combined what seemed right into the Usui System of Healing. This is apparent in the "Original Reiki Ideals" which we now know came from the Meiji Emperor. This is indicated in the inscription on the Usui Memorial, located at Saihoji Temple. The inscription also indicates Usui Sensei studied many things, but his life was not going well when he decided to go to Mt. Kurama to meditate for answers. Perhaps he was looking for the kind of personal transformation for which the mountain is noted and for help in healing his life. It seems he did what many of us have done when our lives have not gone well and we have looked to the spiritual for answers and healing. He opened himself to the Higher Power and not only received a healing for himself, but a way to help others.

Mt. Kurama is covered with giant cedar trees. As we hiked upward, we passed through a section of the trail near the top of the mountain covered with roots, and we thought, yes, the roots of Reiki. At the top of the mountain there is a quiet place with a small shrine called Okunoin Mao-den where Mao-son is said to have descended. Behind the shrine protected by an iron fence is the old cedar tree said to contain the spirit of Mao-son. This area is very calm and has the sound of running water and wind blowing through the trees. We spent a long time here meditating and giving Reiki treatments and attunements to each other.

The Usui Memorial - Answers Carved in Stone

With the help of Arjava Petter, we found the memorial dedicated to Usui Sensei, the founder of the Reiki healing system. It is located at the Saihoji Temple in the Suginami district of Tokyo. The memorial was created by the Usui Shiki Reiki Ryoho in 1927, shortly after Usui Sensei's transition, and is still maintained by the Usui Shiki Reiki Ryoho. This was verified by officials of the Saihoji Temple where the memorial is located. We were surprised that the Usui Shiki Reiki Ryoho still exists because part of the "traditional" story was that all the members of this group died in the war or had stopped using Reiki and that Mrs. Takata was the only remaining teacher of the Usui system in the world. We now know the Usui Shiki Reiki Ryoho has always existed since Usui Sensei's time and it still exists today.

The memorial consists of a large monolith about four feet wide and ten feet tall. On it, written in old-style Japanese kanji, is a description of Usui Sensei's life and his discovery and use of Reiki. It is located in a public cemetery at the Saihoji Temple next to Usui Sensei's gravestone where his ashes, along with those of his wife and son, have been placed. The inscription on the memorial stone was written by Mr. Okata, who is believed to have been a member of the Usui Shiki Reiki Ryoho, and Mr. Ushida, who became president after Usui Sensei died. There are many important and interesting details included in the inscription. (See Chapter 1.)

We went to the memorial site with flowers and we burned some sage there. A butterfly came and landed on the flowers we brought and it felt very peaceful as we drew all the Usui Reiki symbols and sent Reiki to Usui Sensei. We held hands and prayed for Reiki and Usui Sensei to guide us in writing this and sharing a more accurate understanding of Reiki worldwide. We asked for this new information to help unite all Reiki practitioners in harmony and to inspire them to use Reiki to heal each other, all people of the world, and the Earth as a whole. While meditating, we became aware of Usui Sensei with a bright light all around him. We felt he was very happy that an image of his memorial would be seen by so many and that a clearer understanding of how he practiced Reiki would become known.

In Japan Fees for Treatment Are Optional

Shizuko Akimoto shared additional information about Usui Sensei and the history of Reiki. According to her research with Fumio Ogawa and other members of the Usui Shiki Reiki Ryoho, there was never a mandatory fee for Reiki treatments. Dr. Hayashi charged whatever people could pay and if they were poor, he treated them for free. His Reiki business was not lucrative, but was done out of a desire to help people. Many of his students received their Reiki training in return for working at his clinic. If Usui Sensei became popular helping people who suffered from the Tokyo earthquake, as it states on his memorial, it is likely that he, too, did not insist on everyone paying a fee for his treatments but, like Dr. Hayashi, must have treated many for free.

There is no title of "Grand Master" or "Lineage Bearer" in the organization started by Usui Sensei.

The high fees for Master training charged by some in the West are not a requirement of the Usui Shiki Reiki Ryoho. Also, Usui Sensei and Dr. Hayashi are known to have given out class manuals to their students, thus removing another obstacle to learning Reiki - the requirement of a perfect memory! We have received a copy of one of Dr. Hayashi's Reiki manuals and have translated it. It is a description of various illnesses and the hand positions to treat them.

Since Reiki was not a lucrative business, some of Dr. Hayashi's students were forced to stop practicing Reiki due to a lack of adequate income. This suggests that a middle financial path may be more appropriate. A middle path allows one to charge reasonable fees so that one can earn a living, yet be able to lower fees when appropriate or charge nothing for those unable to pay. This allows people to dedicate their life to doing Reiki full-time, thus creating more adept healers who are able to help more people.

The Lineage of Usui Sensei

According to Arjava Petter, there is no title of "Grand Master" or "Lineage Bearer" in the organization started by Usui Sensei. The person in charge of the Usui Shiki Reiki Ryoho is the president. Usui Sensei was the first president of the organization. Since then, there have been five successive presidents: Mr. J. Ushida, Mr. Ilichi Taketomi, Mr. Yohiharu Watanabe, Mr. Toyoichi Wanami, and the current president, Ms. Kimiko Koyama. Dr. Hayashi was a respected teacher, but was never president. According to Rick Rivard, the current president Ms. Koyama is 92 and learned Reiki around the age of 21. Although she was a contemporary of Dr. Mikao Usui, she never met him. She learned Reiki from her late husband. When her husband was offered but turned down the position as head of the society, Ms. Koyama accepted the responsibility. Ms. Koyama is reportedly able to tell where an illness or injury is simply by watching as you enter the room. She treats clients in a reclining chair and receives inner messages that guide her hands during a session. She has developed tremendous healing skills as one would expect from the head of the Usui Shiki Reiki Ryoho.

Language and cultural differences along with a reluctance on the part of the Usui Shiki Reiki Ryoho to speak with Western

Reiki practitioners has restricted our communication. This is why information about the original Usui Reiki organization has taken so long to surface in the West. However, some communication has occurred and a breakthrough is expected soon as the inscription on the Usui Memorial states it is Usui Sensei's wish that Reiki be spread throughout the world.

Helping Others Is What Reiki is All About

This new information about Reiki confirms what many of us have intuitively known all along – the main focus of Reiki is to help others, and because of this there is no need to always require payment for treatments or for training if the person is in need and unable to pay. Mandatory high fees for the teaching level are not a requirement. Moreover, Reiki was not always an oral tradition and both Usui Sensei and Dr. Hayashi had written materials they gave to their students.

Attunements and the practice of Reiki were originally based more on intuitive guidance and intention than on set rules, with the Reiki energy being the defining element. The flexibility of the Usui system makes it broad enough to include a wide range of methods and techniques, thus validating the many different styles being practiced today. We believe the leadership for Reiki lies in Japan where it originated, not in the West.

The Usui Memorial, the information it contains and the energy of Mt. Kurama provide us with an enduring legacy that unites us with Usui Sensei and the spirit of Reiki he rediscovered. This connects us to the roots of the Usui system, to the living energies of its origin. The Usui Memorial with its inscription can provide a focal point for all Reiki groups and a common link that can help to heal the fragmentation and competitiveness which have developed in the West.

Indications of other important discoveries have also made themselves known. These include written materials from Usui Sensei and others. More open communication is likely to occur with members of the Usui Shiki Reiki Ryoho including the president, and is bound to reveal additional useful information.

This is the most wonderful time for Reiki in the West now that we are finally learning the real story of Reiki. Many are feeling a wonderful sense of coming home. May we all share in the joy of these new discoveries and allow them to inspire and empower our Reiki practice.

[1] The lineage of both Fumio Ogawa and Tsutomo Oishi is the same: Dr. Mikao Usui, Iichi Taketomi and Keizo Ogawa. Iichi Taketomi eventually became the president of the Usui Shiki Reiki Ryoho. Keizo Ogawa was a good friend of Dr. Usui also and received his Reiki Master initiation from him as well as from Iichi Taketomi.

Appendix B

Reiki in Hospitals

Reiki in Hospitals

by William Lee Rand

At hospitals and clinics across America, Reiki is beginning to gain acceptance as a meaningful and cost-effective way to improve patient care.

"Reiki sessions cause patients to heal faster with less pain," says Marilyn Vega, RN, a private-duty nurse at the Manhattan Eye, Ear and Throat Hospital in New York. "[Reiki] accelerates recovery from surgery, improves mental attitude and reduces the negative effects of medication and other medical procedures."

Vega, a Reiki Master, includes Reiki with her regular nursing procedures. Because the patients like Reiki, she has attracted a lot of attention from other patients through word of mouth, as well as from members of the hospital staff. Patients have asked her to do Reiki on them in the operating and recovery rooms. She has also been asked to do Reiki sessions on cancer patients at Memorial Sloane Kettering Hospital, including patients with bone marrow transplants. Recognizing the value of Reiki in patient care, six doctors and twenty-five nurses have taken Reiki training with her.

America's Interest in Complementary Health Care

The general public is turning with ever increasing interest to complementary health care, including Reiki. In fact, a study conducted by David M. Eisenberg, M.D. of Boston's Beth Israel Hospital found that one in every three Americans has used such care, spending over 14 billion out-of-pocket dollars on alternative health care in 1990 alone![1]

Reiki is also gaining wider acceptance in the medical establishment. Hospitals across the country are incorporating it into their roster of patient services, often with their own Reiki-trained physicians, nurses and support staff.

Why Hospitals Like Reiki

Hospitals are undergoing major changes. They are experiencing a need to reduce costs and at the same time improve patient care. Under the old medical model based on expensive medication and technology, this posed an unsolvable dilemma. Not so with Reiki and other complementary modalities. Reiki requires no technology at all and many of its practitioners offer their services for free. Reiki is therefore a very good way to improve care while cutting costs.

Julie Motz, a Reiki trained healer, has worked with Mehmet Oz, M.D., a noted cardiothoracic surgeon at Columbia Presbyterian Medical Center in New York. Motz uses Reiki and other subtle energy techniques to balance the patients' energy during operations. She has assisted Dr. Oz in the operating room during open heart surgeries and heart transplants. Motz reports that none of the eleven heart patients so treated experienced the usual post-operative depression, the bypass patients had no post-operative pain or leg weakness; and the transplant patients experienced no organ rejection.

An article in the Marin Independent Journal[2] follows Motz's work at the Marin General Hospital in Marin County, California, just north of San Francisco. There Motz has used subtle energy healing techniques with patients in the operating room. She makes a point of communicating caring feelings and positive thoughts to the patients, and has been given grants to work with mastectomy patients in particular.

David Guillion, M.D., an oncologist at Marin General, has stated: "I feel we need to do whatever is in our power to help the patient. We provide state of the art medicine in our office, but healing is a multi-dimensional process . . . I endorse the idea that there is a potential healing that can take place utilizing energy."

The Tucson Medical Center's Reiki Clinic

The Reiki Clinic at the Tucson Medical Center (TMC) in Arizona has a team of Reiki practitioners who give Reiki to patients in their rooms. The program is administered by Sally Soderlund, RN, who is the Support Services Coordinator for Oncology. Arlene Siegel, who has been with the program from the beginning, runs the monthly support meetings for the Reiki volunteers.

The TMC program started in May 1995. Three Reiki Masters invited members of the Tucson Reiki community to help them start a Reiki clinic, but lacked the funds for a location. In the process of trying to solve this problem, they contacted Sandy Haywood, the hospital administrator at TMC, and offered to provide Reiki sessions for the hospital patients. Haywood had a supportive attitude toward complementary care and made it possible for the hospital Reiki program to get started.

The program first began in the Cancer Care Unit, but has since expanded to many other areas in the hospital. At first, the attending physician had to give permission for Reiki to be provided. This has changed, and now the attending nurse makes the request. Reiki sessions are given by two-person teams as this creates a feeling of safety and confidence for both the patients and the practitioners. Patients must sign a consent form and sessions are given in their rooms while they are in bed.

It is up to the Reiki team to explain Reiki to each patient before giving the treatment. They have found this usually works best by first taking a few minutes to introduce themselves and get to know the patient, then explain the work they do.

They have found it best not to use the word "Reiki" at first when describing how they can help, but to talk about healing energy. They explain how healing energy exists in the body but is depleted when a person is sick, and they describe their work as helping to increase the patient's healing energy supply. Later, after trust has been gained, they explain more about the technique and that it is called Reiki. They also play special healing music during the Reiki session.

Volunteers at the Reiki clinic have found it helpful not to use metaphysical terms when talking to patients or to hospital staff about Reiki. Terms like aura, chakras, energy bodies, etc. tend to cause confusion and mistrust. It works better to explain Reiki in everyday terms by simply saying that touching is something everyone needs and enjoys. They also found that describing their work as Reiki *treatments* tended to create some fear, whereas calling them Reiki *sessions* worked much better.

When new Reiki volunteers come in, Soderlund has them fill out a detailed questionnaire and sign a release form. Volunteers must agree not to solicit Reiki sessions from the patients for treatment outside the hospital. Then they are assigned to work with an experienced two-person Reiki team in a process they call *shadowing*. After six shadowing sessions, Soderlund goes over administrative procedures with them, giving information about how the hospital works and explaining how to interact with the hospital staff and the patients. They are also told how to deal with various issues that might arise. Then they team up with another veteran volunteer or another new volunteer like themselves to form a new two-person team. There are about twenty volunteers in the program now with two to four giving treatments at any one time.

Siegel runs monthly meetings for the Reiki volunteers. At the meetings they set goals, share experiences and go over policy such as dress code and other guidelines on conduct. They also do role playing where they develop new ways to respond to patients' questions or comments. At the meetings they have developed a questionnaire to keep track of patients' progress after receiving Reiki.

Siegel believes that each patient requires a unique response. Most of the patients are very sick, some are dying, but they all respond to their conditions differently. Conditions treated at the Reiki Clinic include cancer, pain, chronic conditions, and post-operative surgery (they also deal with childbirth).

Siegel says that "from the time we enter the patients room, the patients' best interests are uppermost in our minds. We take time to establish rapport, listen to them describe their condition and make them as comfortable as possible. Then, as we become channels for Reiki to do its work and the Reiki begins to flow, the real reason for our presence becomes apparent." She says people volunteer because of the feelings they have in their hearts and other spiritual experiences they receive by helping those in need.

The main reason the program is successful is that the patients like Reiki and request it. The patients enjoy the sessions and request more after their first experience. Some have reported spiritual experiences. Nurses also report that Reiki has positive effects on their patients including reduced pain, increased relaxation, better sleep, better patient cooperation and increased appetite. The program has been well-received by other members of the hospital staff who sense the value of Reiki and accept that it is fulfilling an important aspect of hospital care.[3]

Reiki at Portsmouth Regional Hospital

Patricia Alandydy is an RN and a Reiki Master. She is the Assistant Director of Surgical Services at Portsmouth Regional Hospital in Portsmouth, New Hampshire. With the support of her Director Jocclyn King and CEO William Schuler, she has made Reiki services available to patients within the Surgical Services Department. This is one of the largest departments in the hospital and includes the operating room, Central Supply, the Post Anesthesia Care Unit, the Ambulatory Care Unit and the Fourth Floor where patients are admitted after surgery. During telephone interviews with pre-op patients, Reiki is offered along with many other services. If patients request it, Reiki is then incorporated into their admission the morning of surgery, and an additional fifteen-to-twenty-minute session is given prior to their transport to the operating room. Reiki has also been done in the operating room at Portsmouth Regional Hospital.

Reiki sessions are given by twenty members of the hospital staff whom Patricia has trained in Reiki. These include RN's, physical therapists, technicians and medical records and support staff. Reiki services began in April 1997 and 400 patients have received sessions to date either pre- or post-operatively.

"It has been an extremely rewarding experience," Alandydy says, "to see Reiki embraced by such a diverse group of people and spread so far and wide by word of mouth, in a positive light. Patients many times request a Reiki [session] based on the positive experience of one of their friends. It has also been very revealing to see how open-minded the older patient population is to try Reiki. In the hospital setting Reiki is presented as a technique which reduces stress and promotes relaxation, thereby enhancing the body's natural ability to heal itself."

The Reiki practitioners do not add psychic readings or other new-age techniques to the Reiki sessions, but just do straight Reiki. Because of these boundaries, and the positive results that have been demonstrated, Reiki has gained credibility with the physicians and other staff members. It is now being requested from other care areas of the hospital to treat anxiety, chronic pain, cancer and other conditions.

Alandydy, with her partner Greda Cocco, also manage a hospital-supported Reiki clinic through their business called Seacoast Complementary Care, Inc. The clinic is open two days a week and staffed by fifty trained Reiki volunteers, half of whom come from the hospital staff and the rest from the local Reiki community. They usually have thirteen to seventeen Reiki tables in use at the clinic with one or two Reiki volunteers per table. The clinic treats a wide range of conditions including HIV, pain, and side-effects from chemotherapy and radiation. Some patients are referred by hospital physicians and some come by word of mouth from the local community. They are charged a nominal fee of $10.00 per session. The clinic is full each night and often has a waiting list.[4]

The California Pacific Medical Center's Reiki Program

The California Pacific Medical Center is one of the largest hospitals in northern California. Its Health and Healing Clinic, a branch of the Institute for Health and Healing, provides care for both acute and chronic illness using a wide range of complementary care including Reiki, Chinese medicine, hypnosis, biofeedback, acupuncture, homeopathy, herbal therapy, nutritional therapy and aromatherapy. The clinic has six treatment rooms and is currently staffed by two physicians, Mike Cantwell, M.D. and Amy Saltzman, M.D.. Cantwell, a pediatrician specializing in infectious diseases, is also a Reiki Master with training in nutritional therapy. Saltzman specializes in internal medicine and has training in mindfulness meditation, acupuncture and nutritional therapy. Other professionals are waiting to join the staff, including several physicians.

The doctors at the clinic work with the patients and their referring physicians to determine what complementary modalities will be appropriate for the patient. A detailed questionnaire designed to provide a holistic overview of the patient's condition is used to help decide the course of treatment. The questionnaire involves a broad range of subjects including personal satisfaction with relationships including friends and family, body image, job, career, and spirituality. The clinic is very popular and currently has a waiting list of more than 100 patients.

Dr. Cantwell provides one to three hour long Reiki sessions, after which he assigns the patient to a Reiki II internist who continues to provide Reiki sessions outside the clinic. Patients who continue to respond well to the Reiki treatments are referred for Reiki training so they can do Reiki self-treatments on a continuing basis.

Dr. Cantwell states: "I have found Reiki to be useful in the treatment of acute illnesses such as musculoskeletal injury/pain, headache, acute infections, and asthma. Reiki is also useful for patients with chronic illnesses, especially those associated with chronic pain."

At this point, Reiki is not covered by insurance at the clinic, but Dr. Cantwell is conducting clinical research in the hope of convincing insurance companies that complementary care is viable and will save them money.[5]

More MD's and Nurses Practicing Reiki

Mary Lee Radka is a Reiki Master and an RN who has the job classification of Nurse-Healer because of her Reiki skills. She teaches Reiki classes to nurses and other hospital staff at the University of Michigan Hospital in Ann Arbor. She also uses Reiki with most of her patients. She has found Reiki to produce the best results in reducing pain and stress, improving circulation and eliminating nerve blocks.

Reiki Master Nancy Eos, MD, was a member of the teaching staff of the University of Michigan Medical School. As an emergency-room physician, she treated patients with Reiki along with standard medical procedures.

"I can't imagine practicing medicine without Reiki," Eos says. "With Reiki all I have to do is touch a person. Things happen that don't usually happen. Pain lessens in intensity. Rashes fade. Wheezing gives way to breathing clearly. Angry people begin to joke with me."

In her book *Reiki and Medicine*[6] she includes descriptions of using Reiki to treat trauma, heart attack, respiratory problems, CPR, child abuse, allergic reactions and other emergency-room situations. Dr. Eos now maintains a family practice at Grass Lake Medical Center and is an admitting-room physician at Foote Hospital in Jackson, Michigan, where she continues to use Reiki in conjunction with standard medical procedures. According to Dr. Eos, there are at least five other physicians at Foote hospital who have Reiki training along with many nurses.

Libby Barnett and Maggie Chambers are Reiki Masters who have treated patients and given Reiki training to staff members in over a dozen New England hospitals. They teach Reiki as complementary care and the hospital staff they have trained add Reiki to the regular medical procedures they administer to their patients. Their book *Reiki Energy Medicine*[7] describes their experiences. One of the interesting things they recommend is creating hospital "Reiki Rooms," staffed by volunteers, where patients as well as hospital staff can come to receive Reiki treatments. Bettina Peyton, MD, one of the physicians Libby and Maggie have trained states: "Reiki's utter simplicity, coupled with its potentially powerful effects, compels us to acknowledge the concept of a universal healing energy."

Anyone interested in bringing Reiki into hospitals is encouraged to do so. The hospital setting where there are so many people in real need is a wonderful place to offer Reiki. The experiences and recommendations in this article should provide a good starting point for developing Reiki programs in your area.

[1] Eisenberg, David, et al. "Unconventional Medicine in the United States." *New England Journal of Medicine* 328, no. 4 (1993), 246-52.

[2] Ashley, Beth. "Healing hands," *Marin Independent Journal*, May 11, 1997.

[3] If you have additional questions about the Reiki Clinic at TMC, call Sally Soderlund at (520) 324-2900.

[4] If you have questions for Patricia, you can contact her at 1-603-433-5175. There may be a slight delay in response because of her busy schedule, but she will get back to you.

[5] Mike Cantwell, M.D. can be reached at 1-415-923-3503.

[6] Unfortunately, her book is no longer in print.

[7] Barnett, Libby and Maggie Chambers with Susan Davidson, *Reiki Energy Medicine*, Healing Arts Press, Rochester, Vermont, 1996. Libby and Maggie are at the Reiki Healing Connection, 1-603-654-2787.

Appendix C

Reiki Training and Licensing through the International Center for Reiki Training

Reiki I and II

Reiki I and II are taught together during a two day weekend intensive. All attunements are given. All the information and techniques in this manual are covered including:

- ✡ The Reiki hand positions
- ✡ Giving a complete Reiki treatment
- ✡ Using Reiki for specific conditions
- ✡ The Reiki II symbols and how to use them
- ✡ Using Reiki to heal unwanted habits
- ✡ Distant healing
- ✡ Scanning
- ✡ Beaming

The class is a combination of lecture, discussion and experience. Practice time includes giving and receiving a complete Reiki treatment using all the hand positions, practicing self treatment, scanning others, beaming, using the Second Degree symbols and sending Reiki to others at a distance.

While practice takes place during the class, it is expected that you will set aside additional time to practice after the class is over. Please commit to this additional time which should be one evening a week for several weeks or its equivalent, to practice Reiki with one or more people from your Reiki class or with members of your family or friends. This additional practice is necessary to gain the experience and confidence you need to fully utilize Reiki training.

After completing the class, nurses, massage therapists and body workers are eligible for CEU credits.

Cost $310.00(may vary outside USA)

Advanced Reiki Training

This is a one day intensive class. It includes:

- ✡ The Usui Master attunement which increases the strength of your Reiki energy.
- ✡ The Usui Master symbol which increases the effectiveness of the Reiki II symbols and can be used for healing.
- ✡ Reiki meditation that strengthens the mind and expands the consciousness.
- ✡ Advanced techniques for using Reiki to solve problems and achieve goals.
- ✡ Using Reiki to protect yourself and others.
- ✡ The use of crystals and stones with Reiki.
- ✡ How to make a Reiki grid that will continue to send Reiki to yourself and others after it is charged.
- ✡ Reiki aura clearing that allows you to remove negative psychic energy from yourself and others and send it to the light.
- ✡ A guided meditation that introduces you to your Reiki guides, from whom you receive healing and information.
- ✡ An exercise for those planning to take Reiki III/Master training.

Cost $205.00(may vary outside USA)

A 20 page class manual is included. Note: You must take ART if you want to take Reiki III/Master. This class is often taught with Reiki III as a three day intensive.

Reiki III/Master Training

This is a two day intensive class. It includes:

- ✡ The complete Reiki III Usui/Tibetan Master attunement.
- ✡ Instruction on how to do all Reiki attunements including the Master attunement.
- ✡ The Healing attunement as described.
- ✡ The Usui system of attunements as well as the Usui/Tibetan system used by the Center.
- ✡ Two additional Tibetan symbols for a total of six.
- ✡ Lots of practice time doing attunements.
- ✡ How to give yourself attunements.
- ✡ How to send attunements to others at a distance.
- ✡ Advanced Reiki meditation that harmonizes the energy of the chakras.
- ✡ The values and spiritual orientation of a true Reiki Master.
- ✡ Review of all previous material.

Instruction is given on the Usui system of attunements as well as the Tibetan system and several variations. Over half the class time is used for practice so students become confident in administering Reiki attunements. Students practice giving attunements on each other so that each student receives many attunements. The Healing attunement is given and received by all students. This class is a powerful healing experience. A 62 page class manual is included that gives detailed steps for giving all the attunements. While the content of the class enables anyone to pass on the ability to do Reiki and to teach if one chooses, many take the class for their own use or to use with family and friends.

Cost $620.00(may vary outside USA)

Karuna Reiki® Training

This is an advanced class and is taught only to Reiki Masters. Karuna is a Sanskrit word that means compassionate action. This healing system was developed by William Lee Rand. It has been thoroughly tested and found to be very effective. In fact, most Reiki masters find it to be more powerful than Usui Reiki. It is the next step after Usui Master training. It contains two levels, eight practitioner symbols and four master symbols. Each symbol has a specific purpose and effect.

A description of the four Karuna I symbols is given here: The first symbol prepares the client to receive deep healing and is also useful with past life issues. The second symbol heals deeply seated issues including unconscious patterns, child and sexual abuse, shadow self issues and can release the cause of psychic and psychological attack. It also works with karmic issues on a cellular level. The third symbol fills the client with love and can be used to heal relationships, stop bad habits and create good ones, heal addictions and develop compassion. The fourth symbol grounds the client by opening the lower chakras and strengthening ones connection to the Earth. It also clears the mind, creates determination and helps manifest goals. It can be used at the end of a session to integrate and complete the healing process.

The Karuna II symbols are of a higher vibration and more powerful than those of Karuna I. They help connect directly with the Higher Self and work on a deeper level. While they have specific purposes explained in class, the experience of their energy allows intuitive guidance in their use. Both levels are taught during a three day weekend class. Upon completing the training, you will be able to practice, initiate and teach both levels of Karuna Reiki®. A 45 page manual and certificate is included.

Cost $825.00(may vary outside USA)

Preparing for a Reiki Attunement

A Reiki attunement is a process of empowerment that opens your crown, heart and palm chakras and connects you to the unlimited source of Reiki energy. During the attunement, and for a time after, changes will be made by the attunement energy to enable you to channel Reiki. These changes take place metaphysically in the chakras and aura and also in the physical body. An emotional as well as a physical toxic release can take place as part of this clearing process.

In order to improve the results you receive during the attunement, a process of purification is recommended. This will allow the attunement energies to work more efficiently and create greater benefits for you. *The following steps are optional.* Follow them if you feel guided to do so.

1. Refrain from eating meat, fowl or fish for three days prior to the attunement. These foods often contain drugs in the form of penicillin and female hormones, and toxins in the form of pesticides and heavy metals, that make your system sluggish and throw it out of balance.

2. Consider a water or juice fast for one to three days especially if you already are a vegetarian or have experience with fasting.

3. Minimize your use of coffee and caffeine drinks or stop completely. They create imbalances in the nervous and endocrine systems. Use no caffeine drinks on the day of the attunement.

4. Use no alcohol for at least three days prior to the attunement.

5. Minimize or stop using sweets. Eat no chocolate.

6. If you smoke, cut back, and smoke as little as possible on the day of the attunement.

7. Meditate for half an hour each day for at least a week using a style you know or simply spend this time in silence.

8. Reduce or eliminate time watching TV, listening to the radio, and reading newspapers.

9. Go for quiet walks, spend time with nature, and get moderate exercise.

10. Give more attention to the subtle impressions and sensations within and around you; contemplate their meaning.

11. Release all anger, fear, jealousy, hate, worry, etc. up to the light. Create a sacred space within and around you.

12. A Reiki attunement is an initiation into a sacred metaphysical order that has been present on Earth for thousands of years. By receiving an attunement you will become part of a group of people who are using Reiki to heal themselves and each other, and who are working together to heal the Earth. By becoming part of this group, you will also be receiving help from the Reiki guides and other spiritual beings who are working toward these goals.

Class Schedule

Reiki classes are taught under Center auspices all over the U.S. as well as in other countries. If you are interested in attending a class, please call us or check the schedule on the back of the *Reiki News*. If you would like to sponsor a class in your area please contact the Center.

Licensing

You do not have to become licensed to teach Reiki. Anyone who has taken Reiki I & II and taken time to master the use of the symbols and healing techniques can take ART/III Master training. This includes those who have studied with other teachers or schools. There are no other requirements.

After taking ART/III Master training, you will have the basic requirements necessary to teach all levels of Reiki as an independent Reiki Master. You can begin teaching on your own or you may choose to continue your training and become a Center Licensed Reiki Master Teacher. Licensing has many benefits.

Benefits of Center Licensing

The Center Licensed Teachers Program is briefly described in Chapter 3. By becoming a Center Licensed Reiki Master Teacher, the additional studies, coaching, encouragement and co-teaching will make you more qualified to teach Reiki. We will then be able to list your classes in our newsletter and on our web site and refer students to you. Our newsletter currently goes out to 72,000 people and our web site receives 2,800 visits a week! As a Center Licensed Teacher, your classes will qualify to give Continuing Education Credits (CEU's) to nurses, massage therapists, body workers and athletic trainers, and we are continuing to acquire CEU's for other disciplines as well. We will also be able to work more closely with you and help promote your classes. It is our intention that all our Licensed Teachers do well.

Please note that you do not have to become Licensed by the Center in order to teach Reiki. You can do so on your own as an Independent Reiki Master Teacher after taking the ART/III/

Master training. Some students choose to teach on their own at first and then become licensed through the Center. If, after taking the ART/III Master class, questions come up about how to practice or teach Reiki, do not hesitate to call or write the Center as we are more than happy to help you.

Center Licensed Teachers Booklet

If you are interested in learning more about our Center Licensed Teachers program, send for our Center Licensed Teachers Booklet. It contains all the necessary forms and completely explains our program.

CP-609 $5.00

Reiki Web Site

We have a 125+ page Internet Web Site. It contains lots of valuable information about Reiki including most of the articles from back issues of the *Reiki News*, the Global Healing Network, a listing of our classes world-wide and much more.

Web site address **http://www.reiki.org**
E-mail **Center@reiki.org**

The International Center for Reiki Training
Phone (800) 332-8112, (248) 948-8112
Fax (248) 948-9534

Client Information Form

I, the undersigned, understand that the Reiki session given is for the purpose of stress reduction and relaxation. I understand very clearly that a Reiki session is not a substitute for medical or psychological diagnosis and treatment. Reiki practitioners do not diagnose conditions, nor do they prescribe or perform medical treatment, nor prescribe substances, nor interfere with the treatment of a licensed medical professional. It is recommended that I see a licensed physician or licensed health care professional for any physical or psychological ailment I have.

Signature ____________________ Date ____________________

Print Name ____

Address ____

City ____

State/Country ____________________ Zip ______________

Phone ____

Progress and Treatment Record		
Date	Fee	Remarks

The Beaming Reiki Masters

This picture was taken at a Karuna Reiki® class held at the Center. The class members used the distant symbol and projected Karuna symbols into the camera, intending that all who see the resultant picture would receive Reiki energy. Clairvoyant observation indicates that Reiki energy comes directly from the Reiki source and does not pass through those in the picture. Place it in front of you or carry it with you. It can be used by itself or in conjunction with hands on Reiki or other healing or meditation techniques. Feel free to experiment with it and make copies of this page to give to friends.

Takata's Masters

Mrs. Takata initiated twenty-two Reiki Masters between 1970 and her transition in 1980. Below is a list of the Reiki Masters she initiated. This is the list she gave to her sister before she passed through transition.

George Araki
Barbara McCullough
Beth Gray
Ursula Baylow
Paul Mitchell
Iris Ishikura (deceased)
Fran Brown
Barbara Weber Ray
Ethel Lombardi
Wanja Twan
Virginia Samdahl
Phyllis Lei Furumoto
Dorothy Baba (deceased)
Mary McFadyen
John Gray
Rick Bockner
Bethal Phaigh (deceased)
Harry Kuboi
Patricia Ewing
Shinobu Saito
Takata's Sister
Barbara Brown

Reading List

Arnold, L. & Nevius, S. *The Reiki Handbook*. Harrisburg, PA: PSI Press, 1982.

Baginski, B. & Sharamon, S. *Reiki: Universal Life Energy*. Mendocino, CA: Life Rhythm Pub., 1985.

Brennan, B. *Hands of Light*. New York: Bantam Books, 1988.

Brown, F. *Living Reiki: Takata's Teachings*. Life Rhythm, 1992.

Clay, M. *The Challenge to Teach Reiki*, Australia: Clay, 1992.

Clay, M. *One Step Forward for Reiki*, Australia: Clay, 1992.

Gerber, R. *Vibrational Medicine*. Santa Fe, NM: Bear & Co., 1988.

Gleisner, E. *Reiki In Everyday Living*. White Feather Press, 1992.

Haberly, H. *Reiki: Hawayo Takata's Story*. Garrett Park, MD: Archedigm Pub., 1990.

Heinz, S. *Healing Magnetism*. Your Beach, Maine: Samuel Weiser, Inc., 1987.

Hochhuth, K. *Practical Guide to Reiki an Ancient Healing Art*, Victoria, Australia: Gemcrafters Books, 1993.

Horan, P. *Empowerment through Reiki*. Wilmot, WI: Lotus Light Pub., 1990.

Jarrel, D. *Reiki Plus First* Degree. Edenton, NC: Reiki Plus Institute, 1984.

Jarrel, D. *Reiki Plus Professional Practitioners Manual for Second Degree*. Edenton, NC: Reiki Plus Institute, 1992.

Krieger, D. *The Therapeutic Touch*. New York: Prentice Hall Press, 1986.

Kunz, D. *Spiritual Aspects of the Healing Arts*. Wheaton, IL: The Theosophical Publishing House.

Kushi, M. & Oredson, O. *Macrobiotic Palm Healing*. New York: Japan Pub., Inc., 1988.

Lubeck, W. *The Complete Reiki Handbook*. Twin Lakes, WI: Lotus Light Publications, 1994.

Lugenbeel, B. *Virginia Samdahl: Reiki Master Healer*. Norfolk, VA: Gunwald and Radcliff Pub., 1984.

Mitchell, P. *The Blue Book*. Cataldo, ID: The Reiki Alliance, 1985.

Petter, F. *Reiki Fire*. Twin Lakes, WI: Lotus Light Pub., 1997.

Ray, B. *The Reiki Factor*. St. Petersburg, FL: Radiance Associates, 1983.

Stewart, J.C. *The Reiki Touch*. Houston, TX: The Reiki Touch, Inc., 1989.

Appendix D

Books, Tapes, Supplies and Other Resources

Audio Tapes

Reiki Symposium - New York City, 1998

This four hour three tape set includes some of the best information on Reiki coming from top authorities in the field.

Tape One:

• Reiki - An Overview by Louisiana Zinn • Reiki, In Continuing Education by Diane Alther • Reiki, For a Strong Economy and Healthy Planet by Lisa Berkley • Reiki and Medicine by Kathleen Tracey Kardaras

Tape Two:

• Reiki - A New Direction by William Lee Rand • Creating Harmony in Your Reiki Community by Laura Ellen Gifford

Tape Three:

• A Reiki Panel Discussion with William Lee Rand, Laura Ellen Gifford, Diane Alther, Lisa Berkley, Kathleen Tracey Kardaras and Louisiana Zinn.

Tape #CT100 $19.95 postpaid

Meet Your Reiki Guides

There are spiritual beings who are Reiki Masters. They can provide guidance as you give Reiki treatments and also guide you on your path through life. They can add their Reiki energy to yours to increase the effectiveness of a treatment and they can send you love, protection and healing throughout the day. The more you are aware of them, the more they can help. This audio cassette tape is a guided meditation that gradually increases your level of consciousness so you can communicate more effectively with your Reiki guides. You can ask questions and receive guidance and healing. Side Two is a guided meditation that connects you with the energies of the Earth and the Universe. This tape was created by William Lee Rand. **Tape #M102 $12.00 postpaid**

Spiritual Protection and Healing Tape

✡ Creates a protective field of psychic energy around you that prevents negative energy from reaching you.
✡ Transmutes negative energy into healing energy.
✡ Attunes you to your guides and Higher-Self.
✡ Protects from and permanently breaks all curses, hexes and black spells.
✡ Activates The Healing Center Within.
✡ Helps you balance karma, learn life lessons and advance spiritually.

Often, one of the greatest difficulties in life is dealing with negative psychic and psychological energies from other people. Negative psychic energy can come from fellow workers, competitors, friends, relatives and relationships. It is often in the form of irrational anger, hate, envy or fear and is usually unconscious, but can also be consciously and deliberately directed at you.

Negative psychic energy from others can cause stress, nervousness, lack of confidence, weakness, sleeplessness, poor health, aches and pains in your body and energy depletion.

It is no longer necessary to be affected by others' negative energy. The Spiritual Protection and Healing tape uses a form of deep self-hypnosis called spiritual hypnosis to place a protective barrier of psychic healing energy around you that not only prevents negative energy from reaching you but actually transmutes negative energy into healing energy and directs it to heal the cause of the negative energy. In addition, it prevents others from taking your energy, breaks all psychic cords connected to negative sources of influence, places a cloud of healing energy around you, and attunes you to your guides and Higher Self.

Two Effective Tools in One Audio Tape

Spiritual Protection & Healing
and the Healing Center Within
This is a valuable tool to assist those who are
actively walking their spiritual path.

"As I work intensely on my spiritual growth, the clearer my light becomes. As I grow, at times I sense less than light energy directed toward me. The tape by William Rand, "Spiritual Protection and Healing," has been invaluable to me during this time of rapid growth. Not only does it help one create an energy of protection, but it assists in transforming negative energy into healing energy that is redirected to heal the source. This is a most positive tool for protection and healing."

Laura Ellen Gifford, Center Licensed Reiki Master Teacher

The major problems, restrictions and challenging situations in your life contain opportunities for you to grow and develop. Within them are lessons you need to learn to progress on your spiritual path and become fulfilled.

Side Two of this tape forms a powerful connection between your Higher Self and your subconscious mind and establishes The Healing

Center Within. Making use of the great wisdom, love and healing power of the Higher Self, The Healing Center Within knows everything you have ever done, in this life and all your past lives. It knows all about your problems and it knows exactly what you need to do to solve them. It will start a process to completely heal you and guide you on your path of spiritual development as it empowers you to balance your karma and learn your life lessons.

This tape is a breakthrough in spiritual protection and healing. It combines the knowledge and techniques of white magic, neuro-linguistic programming and self-hypnosis. This is a powerful self-hypnosis tape that helps you be more centered, healthy and in touch with your own inner wisdom and personal power regardless of the psychic environment. The effects are post-hypnotic; if listened to regularly, they are continuous.

This deep self-hypnosis tape was developed by William Lee Rand over a period of twenty years. William is a hypnotherapist specializing in spiritual development. In addition he has a background as a past-life therapist, an astrologer, a rebirther, a TM meditator, a Rosicrucian, a fire walker, has worked with a Kahuna in Hawaii, is certified in Neuro-Linguistic Programming, and is a Reiki Master Teacher and founder of the International Center for Reiki Training.

The Reiki Class Tapes

First and Second Degree Training
Three Hours of Reiki Instruction
on Cassette Tape
by William Lee Rand

The tapes include:

- ✡ The history of Reiki
- ✡ The development of the Usui System of Natural Healing
- ✡ The origin of the $10,000 fee
- ✡ What Reiki energy is
- ✡ How Reiki heals
- ✡ The Second Degree symbols, how they work and the many ways to use them
- ✡ The Way of Reiki - A Spiritual Path
- ✡ Questions and answers about Reiki

These tapes were made during actual Reiki classes taught by William Lee Rand. If you feel you may not have gotten the complete Reiki training or if you have questions that have gone unanswered about Reiki, this is the tape set for you. William gives in-depth answers to the most frequently asked questions about Reiki and includes all the information from his Reiki I & II intensive. William was trained by seven Reiki Masters, has thirteen years of experience with Reiki and has taught over 250 Reiki classes in the USA and around the world. Rather than simply accepting the "traditional" information about Reiki, William has done extensive research so that he can bring you a clear understanding of what Reiki is and how to get the best results with it.

Three hours of Reiki instruction on cassette tape.
Three tape set #M230 $29.95

To Order Call:
800-332-8112, or 248-948-8112, Fax 248-948-9534
Major Credit Cards Accepted

The Reiki Table

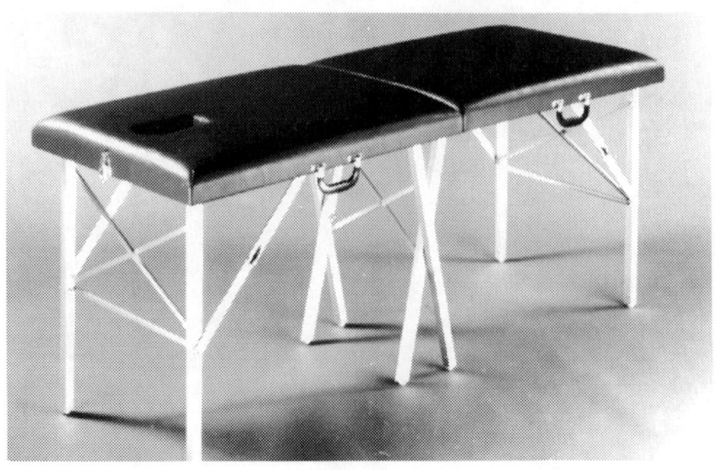

Size: 24" wide 28" high, 72" long with face hole (Folded 24" x 6" x 36")

Colors: Blue Spruce, Wild Plum, Desert Rose, Aspen Tan, Lake Blue, Ginger Bark

Weight: 26 pounds

Guaranteed

If you are not happy with your Reiki table, simply return it in its original condition and packaging, within 30 days, for a refund of the purchase price. The Reiki table is also guaranteed for workmanship and materials. Just return it within 90 days for replacement. Please contact us for a Return Merchandise Authorization number.

We have these tables custom-made for us by one of the best massage table manufacturers in the country. They are strong, yet light and well made. With no cables around the bottom, there is plenty of room for your legs to fit under the table when seated. It is a very comfortable table for Reiki. Its wooden top retains Reiki energy and the metal legs keep the table grounded so that negative energies that are released during a treatment flow away. This is a great table for Reiki that can also be used for massage!

#RT200 Reiki Table Price: $340.00

Please state color when ordering

Deluxe table available, call Center for details

Reiki Hand Positions Poster

This is a poster of the Reiki hand positions for treating both others and yourself. Large enough to see from across the room. Great for your Reiki room.

Size 25" x 38" **#M702 Price: $12.00**

Reiki Class Workbook

This is an 8½" x 11" version of this book, and it is spiral bound to open flat and has larger illustrations. Ideal for use by students in Reiki classes. Purchases of five or more receive a 30 percent discount.

CP401TM $14.95, five or more at $10.47 each

To Order Call:
800-332-8112, or 248-948-8112, Fax 248-948-9534
Major Credit Cards Accepted

Reiki News

The *Reiki News,* a quarterly publication, contains many interesting articles on Reiki that include information on improving your Reiki treatments, using Reiki in conjunction with other healing techniques and developing your Reiki practice. There are also stories written by practitioners and teachers about their personal experiences with Reiki. A list of Center Licensed Teachers and classes world wide is included. The *Reiki News* promotes the idea of global healing through personal transformation, and honors the value created by all Reiki practitioners regardless of their lineage or affiliation.

The *Reiki News* is also a catalog of Reiki products including: Reiki T-shirts & sweat pants, Reiki books and tapes, new age music, Reiki tables, herbs, candles, crystals, Tachyon Healing Tools, and more!

Are Your Usui Reiki Symbols Accurate?

Usui Reiki symbols have traditionally been kept secret. This has its value, but has also helped create a problem.

As the symbols were passed on orally from teacher to student over and over, the lack of a perfect memory on the part of the teachers and other problems allowed the symbols to change. In addition, some teachers channeled new symbols and began teaching them without telling their students they were non-Usui symbols. Because of this, some students are now receiving symbols that look nothing like the symbols taught by Dr. Usui. While it is true that all Reiki symbols work as long as they are empowered by a Reiki attunement, some students have expressed an interest in verifiying the accuracy of their symbols. (The books currently published that include the symbols have not been thoroughly researched and may contain inaccuracies.)

If you have taken a Reiki II or Master class and wonder if you have received the original Usui Reiki symbols, send us a stamped self-addressed envelope and a copy of your Reiki certificate, and we will send you a copy of the original Usui Reiki symbols along with an article about the Reiki symbols.

Index

A

B

C

D

E

F

G

H

I

J

K

L

M

N

O

P-Q

R

S

T

U

V

W

X-Z